Waking Your Dreams

Waking Your Dreams

Unlock the Wisdom of Your Unconscious

Discover your personal imagery.

Meet your authentic self.

Explore beneath the surface of your mind.

Emma Mellon, PhD

Health Communications, Inc.
Deerfield Beach, Florida

www.hcibooks.com

Library of Congress Cataloging-in-Publication Data
is available at the Library of Congress

©2006 Emma Mellon, PhD
ISBN 0-7573-0554-7

Publisher: Health Communications, Inc.
        3201 S.W. 15th Street
        Deerfield Beach, FL 33442-8190

Cover design by Larissa Hise Henoch
Inside book design and formatting by Dawn Von Strolley Grove

For Zachary David

Contents

Introduction ix

1 The Lure of the Dream 1

2 Mysteries of the Dream 17

3 Learning the Language of Dreams 27

4 Entering the Dream 49

5 Reruns, Laughter, Synchronicity and Fear 69

6 Daydreams 87

7 Returning 103

Appendix: Doing Dream Work 115

Reference Reading 118

Acknowledgments 120

Index 121

All clients are composite characters drawn
from my experience and clinical work.
Names and details are changed to preserve confidentiality.

Introduction

This is not a dream dictionary. Dreams will not sit still for that. They are neither disciplined nor singular. They wiggle and tease and stamp their feet and change shape. They won't be trussed in alphabetical order like words.

Dreams don't give themselves away easily. They like to be courted. They want us to spend time with them, to think less and feel more, to imagine and to play.

So, this is not a dictionary. It is an invitation to dream, to spend time in that instinctive world and to learn to move freely between it and what we call the "real" world.

Everyone dreams. Every night. Several times a night. But not everyone remembers the dreams. That can be remedied. Just reading a book about dreams can stimulate dreaming and remembering! In these pages, I'll suggest ways to teach yourself to remember and benefit from your dreams.

We'll enter many dreams and practice speaking their metaphorical language. We will look back at ancient dreams and myths and acquaint ourselves with some of the dreamers who have gone before us. We'll also look at where our dreams originate and how we've come to believe what we do about their meanings.

We will consider the emotionally charged dreams that visit us from time to time: the terrifying, the comic and the blissful. We'll spend some time with that powerful tool, the daydream. And I'll describe ways to integrate the richness of dreams into waking life.

Mostly, I would like to remind you that dreams are real experiences. They take up energy and space in consciousness and are the instinctive point of view in a world where the answer is always expected to be outside: in a leader, a pill, a product, a promise or a doctrine. Dreams draw us down into our mysterious underworld where our humanity has its source, and there, they nourish and change us.

Tonight or tomorrow night or next week, you will have a dream. The images will seem obscure, mad and maybe rude, like the babblings of a fool. You'll be tempted to grab that dream dictionary from the shelf and put all the mystery to rest with a bit of research. Or maybe you'll be tempted to shake off the dream and get on with your life. This book gives you another option.

Love them, hate them, be baffled by them. Your dreams are you.

Emma Mellon, PhD
Treetops, Berwyn, PA
March, 2006

tolerate that first wave of bewilderment. C. G. Jung, the Swiss psychiatrist and dream pioneer, began work with every client's dream by admitting that he had no idea what the dream meant. And there, too, our work begins.

Not knowing creates a psychological tension in us. The brain strains toward clarity and closure and will create an answer rather than remain in limbo. That urge to conclude can create the form of a face in the leaves of a tree or answer a problem before having adequate information. The discomfort of not knowing can also motivate. "I don't know what this dream means" becomes the sound of the mind's gears shifting from realistic to imaginative mode. We can learn to tolerate not knowing and to remind our busy, lightning-fast brains that there are other ways to arrive at knowing besides deductive reasoning.

Dreaming History

Humans have been curious about their dreams for as long as they have dreamed. Robert L. Van de Castle, PhD, writer, dream researcher and dreamer, offers a sweeping study of dreaming in *Our Dreaming Mind*. As he points out, primitive humans may have dreamed the figures found on cave walls. The earliest written dreams come from 3000 BCE Assyria and second-century CE Babylonia. They were gathered by Artemedorus, a Roman soothsayer, who included them in his work, *The Interpretation of Dreams*. Over five thousand years later, Sigmund Freud would use the same title for his masterwork on dreams.

Through the ages, dreams have been explained as everything from brain excretions to side effects of digestion to gifts from the gods. Most striking in dream history is the strong connection between dreams and spirituality. And it is an understandable connection. The

The Arab-Muslim world of the 10th century boasted 7,500 dream interpreters involved in the study and explanation of dreams.

~~ ~~ Robert L. Van de Castle

religious impulse is a core element of the psyche, a channel through which psychic energy is expressed. And dreaming is the voice of the psyche. Dreams and spirituality involve a nonrational dimension, one not visible to the eye. Each uses image extensively. Dreams and spirituality are perceived as a connection to a more powerful entity, larger than humans and, in a way, holding some authority over humans. Both provide access to the numinous, that mysterious power that comes unbidden to touch the heart and soul. So it was inevitable that dreams and religion would intermingle.

Written between 1500 and 1000 BCE, the Vedas, sacred wisdom books of India, address favorable and unfavorable dreams and dream meanings. The Upanishads, Indian philosophical treatises written around 800 BCE, offer several dream theories and set dreaming above waking reality. The dreamer, they say, exists between the waking world and the world beyond and can see both. Mahayana Buddhism sees both waking and dreaming as illusions. The Sufis believe in a third world, a dream world that exists between rationality and sensibility. In the Old Testament, Jacob has a dream in which angels ascend and descend a ladder that leads to heaven and God.

As Van de Castle points out, the ladder is an elegant metaphor for the way dreams connect the human realm with the divine. Also in the Old Testament, Joseph, the son of Jacob, dreams that he is binding sheaves in the fields with his brothers. He sees the sheaves stand, and his brothers'

Many cultures, including Indian, Egyptian and Chinese, believed that the soul left the body during dreams and wandered in the world.

~~ ~~ Van de Castle

sheaves gather round and bow to his. Later, he interprets the Pharaoh's dreams and enables the kingdom to prepare for famine. In the New Testament, another Joseph is visited in a dream and told of his wife's virginal conception of Jesus. Later he is warned in a dream about Herod's plans to kill Jesus, and in another he's told when it is safe to return home.

But if dreams can come from God, they could also be sent by the devil. By the 4th century, the place of dreams in the Christian church had changed. In the official Latin translation of the Bible, the scholar Jerome equated witchcraft with dreams. What followed were centuries of obsession with the evils lurking in human dreams. Demon apparitions, the incubus and the succubus, were said to sexually possess dreamers, so the church prohibited Christians from attending to their dreams. During the Middle Ages in the Western Christian church, reports of prophetic dreams and dreams containing sexual, aggressive or impious themes could earn the dreamer torture or death.

If anyone among you is a prophet, I will make myself known to him in a vision. I will speak to him in a dream.

Numbers 12:6

By the 13th century, the ecclesiastical position had softened somewhat. Thomas Aquinas, in his compilation of Christian theology, warned believers against contacting demons for revelation in dreams but allowed that dreams could also come from God, from physical states, daytime activities or astrological forces. He himself even reported conversing in a dream with Saints Peter and Paul and resolving a block he'd been experiencing with his major work, *Summa Theologica*.

In modern times, dreams have become the study of philosophy, neurology and psychology, and they have also played a significant role in the arts and sciences. Creative activity requires a blend of hard work and letting go into the richness of the unconscious. Often the answer comes in a dream image as it did for Elias Howe, who patented the sewing machine. After years of frustrating work, he dreamed of soldiers carrying spears and he saw that the spears each had a hole near the point. He awoke with the answer to his problem: a needle with its eye by its point.

Jasper Johns' dream about painting an American flag took him from his job as a window dresser in 1950s New York City to the heart of a revolution in painting. Ingmar Bergman used his own dreams in his films *Sawdust and Tinsel* and *Wild Strawberries*. Mary Shelley's nightmare became the novel *Frankenstein*. And *The Strange Case of Dr. Jekyll and Mr. Hyde* came to Robert Louis Stevenson in his sleep. Many other writers, including Jack Kerouac, Robert Penn Warren, Katherine Mansfield and Franz Kafka, report that their dreams gave them stories or helped when the writing was blocked.

> *Muhammad states in the Koran that the science of dreams is "the prime science since the beginning of the world."*
>
> ～ ～ Van de Castle

Even what we call "hard science" has dreams woven deep into its foundation. In 1869, Dmitri Mendeleyev of St. Petersburg, Russia, dreamed of a way of categorizing chemical elements and created the periodic table of elements. In Ghent, Belgium, Friedrich A. von Kekule had been struggling to understand the structure of the benzene molecule. He dreamed of long rows of atoms that formed whirling circles and woke to work out the hexagonal model of the molecule.

As historic figures wrestled with the problems of their time, their dreams influenced the course of history. Harriet Tubman, who brought slaves north on the Underground Railroad, credited dreams with showing her safe routes. The idea of nonviolent strikes, which he led in India in 1919, came to Gandhi in a dream. During World

War II, General George Patton *Hippocrates, father of Greek*
often called his secretary during *medicine, believed dreams*
the night to dictate battle plans *diagnosed physical illness and*
he'd received in dreams. *expressed psychological issues.*
Struggling with the miasma of
the Vietnam War, Lyndon

        — Van de Castle

Johnson dreamed of himself caught in the center of a river, unable to move to either shore. The dream helped Johnson come to the decision not to run for a second term.

On June 28, 1914, Bishop Joseph Lanyi, who had once been the tutor of Archduke Franz Ferdinand of Austria, dreamed of his old pupil. In the dream, Lanyi opened a letter from Ferdinand that announced the fact of Ferdinand's assassination later that same day. It was complete with a sketch of the scene of the shooting. The dream, by its not being reported in time, affected the lives of millions as the assassination of Archduke Ferdinand led to World War I.

Lanyi's was a precognitive dream, that kind of dream that foretells the future. In our own contemporary, ordinary lives and in historic accounts, such dreams are fairly common. The Buddha's mother dreamed of her son's miraculous conception. Muhammad discovered his life's work in a dream and the sacred Koran was revealed to him in dreams. Joseph Smith dreamed in 1820 of The Church of Jesus Christ of Latter-day Saints, which he would go on to establish. Abraham Lincoln dreamed that he would be assassinated and laid in state in the Capitol Rotunda.

Knowing ahead of time and across space is also possible in waking states where the ego has surrendered control to focused imagination. Charlatans and showmen have given psychic ability a bad name, and even reputable psychics receive little respect from the educated public. So it interested me to learn that the U.S. government has done research since the '70s on parapsychological, or psi, activity. Concern that Russian experiments with parapsychology could be used against the United States triggered the research on Remote Viewing at the Stanford Research Institute in Menlo Park, California. On the International Remote Viewing Association Web site, Hal Puthoff, PhD, first director of the program, describes the now declassified studies, which came to show the existence of what they call "psi." Using strict scientific protocol, viewers with various amounts of training were able to successfully identify people and objects at distances ranging from close proximity to the next room to outer space. They found that precognitive knowing was one manifestation of the paranormal modes of perception. They also found that psi operated like the senses in picking up changes in the environment.

Precognitive dreams and Remote Viewing are flashy hints of that other way of knowing also available in our ordinary night dreams and waking intuitions. Perhaps these abilities will gain respectability as times goes on. These transcendent powers of imagination have considerable potential, not as fabrications but as ways of seeing beyond: beyond what we know intellectually, beyond what our other senses tell us is so. Given this proven potential, it's curious that we as a society so underuse dreaming and the powers of imagination.

Imagination is a most secret power that is as much of a cosmic force as of a psychological facility.

Gaston Bachelard

Ah, There's the Rub

Awake and asleep, we yearn for transcendence. We also resist it. We say it's silly, we don't have time, we can't prove what we're experiencing. It makes us uneasy, in the way I might feel trying to shake an insect off my hand: anxious, impatient, distressed, annoyed, just the beginnings of fear of something so "other." I think, "This isn't how it should be. I'm in charge here. Go away. Do what I say."

Charles T. Tart, PhD, is a researcher and scholar who has contributed much to paranormal research. One of his interests is the ambivalence and anxiety triggered in people by the possibility of having psi powers. In a lecture, "Exploring Our Fears of the Paranormal" in an audiotape collection titled "The Future of Energetic Healing," Tart describes finding that individuals feared psi power would be too much responsibility, too scary, too intrusive, and it would make them too vulnerable. How would they manage it without being overwhelmed by it? Though they appreciated the fascinating possibilities of having that power, the actual possession of it took them out of their comfort zones, out to where their usual way of thinking faltered. The same is true with dreams. I believe it would be impossible to overestimate our ambivalence about our psychological, psychic and dream lives. My own reaction to my caveman dream is a very simple example of that. I can feel all my "yes, buts" standing between me and the images, distracting me from the experience of my dream and buffering me from the fact that my waking consciousness is part of something bigger that I need to develop a relationship with.

> *Rather than interpret a dream . . . let a dream interpret us.*
>
>   Thomas Moore

Individual resistance multiplies into cultural resistance. While not condemning or prohibiting dreams and other psychological activities, we as a society marginalize them by putting time and value elsewhere. We concentrate on "getting things done," consuming, conforming, and building isolated controlled pockets of safety and security in a world from which we feel increasingly alienated. We allow our fantasies to be shaped by advertising, politics and religion, by television and radio. The arts subsist on the edge of bankruptcy, while repetitive and violent story lines break the box office. In our increasingly damaged health care system, we short shrift the mind even more than the body. We idolize the intellect, and we believe in getting to answers that can be proven and corroborated. The search for our authentic selves is relegated to "self-help" activities or crisis-driven psychotherapy, which is itself judged frivolous or shameful. We live as if we are static creatures, and we devote our resources to maintaining that sameness. As far as the inner life goes, we seem to believe that no news is good news. The imaginal and unpredictable are classified either as childish and irresponsible or as threats and not as pathways to broader existence.

Anthony Stevens, in *Private Myths: Dreams and Dreaming*, tells a sad and touching story of C. G. Jung's meeting in Africa in the mid-1920s with an Elgonyi medicine man. With great regret, the old man told Jung that his people didn't need their dreams any longer because "the white man, who ruled the earth, knew everything." Over 80 years since Jung's conversation with the Elgonyi medicine man, we've turned even further from the organic dream world. We have come to believe what the old medicine man believed. We think we know, or can know, everything, and we believe that will be enough. We think our dreams can't count in the big scheme of things. Yet, in the face of that social pressure to conform, dreams keep coming to disturb the predictable pace of our lives and balance the solidity of day with the possibilities of night.

> *Myths tell us things about ourselves that we have forgotten to learn in other ways.*
>
> ⟶ ⟶ Berger & Segaller

Dreams are our own personal court jesters. The jester was the king's fool. His job was to tell the truth, to be the king's reality check in the politicized, competitive world of the court. The jester had a mystique. He lured the king back to reality with jokes and puns, warnings and stories. Shakespeare's *King Lear*, the tragic tale of a king who comes too late to wisdom, offers a touching portrait of the relationship between king and jester.

Throughout the play, the fool speaks and Lear argues, ignores, threatens him with punishment but keeps him close. Their relationship isn't easy, but their bond is deep and the jester's love and loyalty for the king are evident. Lear is searching for perfect reverential love from his children, but he comes to learn what the fool has been trying to teach him: that life is not what it seems, and reality is both prickly and kind.

The jester guides the king as dreams lure the dreamer. Even as we argue and resist and push in the opposite direction, the dream world and the unconscious persist as a source of life and wisdom. They offer not the perfect love of Lear's longing, but a fidelity, depth and presence that may be the core of love.

Dream Work Practice

So, here I am with my caveman dream. Join me as I step back into the scene and take another look. Using my imagination—my other way of seeing—I recall the scene in as much detail as I can. I enter as I did the first time and go as slowly as I wish. It's like playing a movie on whatever speed I like. I give myself a minute to settle in. I stand on the sand across the lines from the crouching man. I wait; I try to accept what comes to my mind without censoring, without worrying about getting this right. I'm struck by how focused he is on the parallel lines. They remind me of the sand rakings in Zen gardens, which invite attentiveness and receptivity from meditators.

I feel myself beginning to relax. I look closely at the spheres. They're an inch or so in diameter and black. They look like musket ammunition, and I imagine they would feel hard and heavy in the palm of my hand. I am beginning to feel more interested. There's something soothing about looking down this length of lines, something orderly, earthy and safe. As I let my imagination work, I check my emotional and physical responses.

I am feeling curious, content, secure. My body feels confident, relaxed and a bit excited, even though I still don't know "what it means."

A few deep breaths and I end the dream work for now and reorient myself to the day world. What have I accomplished? Is this just make-believe? I answer the questions that pop up with more questions. What if I didn't respond with judgments? What if I didn't evaluate? What if I admitted to having the experience I've just had and bring it back with me into the day world exactly as it is?

Dreams are the language in which all aspects of a person's individual psychology express themselves in uncensored form.

⭐ ⭐ Berger & Segaller

If I did that, I would notice that my restless intellect followed my imagination onto that beach. I became more comfortable, more curious and open. The scene and the man began to become real. I began to share in the man's experience, its serenity and its captivating simplicity. I saw the worries that agitated the dream-Emma and kept her from entering into the scene. I realized the man posed no threat and had admirable qualities. I practiced being present in the moment, which I had not been able to do originally in the dream.

I've begun to bring into my conscious self a new bit of my unconscious. In small ways, I am changed, added to. My perceptions of this coming day will be colored and informed by this brief encounter. "What it means" has begun to unfold.

Mysteries of the Dream

"Dreams are the voice of our instinctive
animal nature or ultimately the voice of
cosmic matter in us."

—Marie-Louise von Franz

Dream Origins

Where do dreams come from? The truth is, we don't know. But we can imagine. And humans have been imagining the answer to that question ever since they began to reflect on their dreams.

Around 3000 BCE, an Egyptian could have gone to the temple at Memphis and performed rituals to implore the god of dreams to send him a dream. For a Talmudic scholar around 1 BCE, erotic dreams were caused by a hairy demon resembling a goat or by another demon named Lilith, who tortured dreamers who slept alone. In China at that period, the dreamer believed that his soul, the *hun*, separated from the body and visited the land of the dead to communicate with spirits there. In a wonderful Australian Aboriginal myth, dreams come from dreamers who themselves are the dream of the Great Spirit.

An early view of dreams in Greece had an actual god entering through the keyhole and standing at the foot of the bed to present the dream. Hippocrates believed that the soul produced dreams, and Aristotle, observing that animals dreamed, said that dreams originated in the body, triggered by physical conditions. Tertullian, a third-century Roman Catholic priest, added forces of nature, such as weather and astronomical conditions, to the list of dream causes.

The Greeks never spoke of "having" a dream, but of "seeing" one. Dreams were said not only to "visit" the dreamer but to "stand over" him.

~~ ~~ A. Alverez

In the darkness of the Middle Ages, people believed dreams came from the devil. The more enlightened dreamers of the seventeenth and eighteenth centuries were likely to believe their dreams came from their own bodies and personalities. By the nineteenth century, a man musing on last night's dream was likely to think about its origin in his unconscious.

Two Europeans dominated dream work in the twentieth century. Sigmund Freud, a Viennese neurologist, defined an unconscious that flowed under normal daily awareness. He saw the unconscious as a dustbin of dark urges that reflected early developmental crises and showed itself in puzzling eruptions of emotion, slips of the tongue, fantasies and dreams. Freud believed that dreams were suppressed wishes from the unconscious, encoded in symbolic language. A cigar was not usually a cigar. He believed interpreting dreams would cure maladjustment in the patient's current life situation. When he called dreams "the royal road to the unconscious," he was building on knowledge accumulated by dream researchers for thousands of years.

Carl Gustav Jung was a Swiss psychiatrist who also analyzed his clients' dreams. In contrast to Freud, Jung read dreams as comments from the unconscious about the client's present and future. Jung conceptualized the unconscious as the underlying source of life and "potential, a vast reservoir from which our conscious beings draw energy." He believed that a person's true nature emerges as consciousness integrates more and more of what has been unconscious.

For Jung, dream images themselves, and not dreams as symbols, connected the dreamer to her deeper self and to an even deeper level of being he called the collective unconscious. Others have called this realm God or True Nature, or Basic Ground, or Life Energy. It doesn't matter whether you identify it as divinity or electromagnetic energy. It is the life stream that has fed the evolution of our species and contains the history of that evolution. Dreams give us direct access to the unconscious. Everything that it means to be human is there.

Jung saw dreams as nightly opportunities to reconnect with our true nature, to discover aspects of personality that have lived outside consciousness and to bring them into conscious daily awareness.

Psychological and scientific learning about our dream processes continue. Today, dreamers meet in person and online to share and understand their dreams. Organizations, most notably the International Association for the Study of Dreams, hold annual conferences that bring together leaders in the field to discuss aspects of dream life, such as dreams in the grief process, politics and dreams, social justice and dreams, and wartime dreams. In one charming bit of research, Brenda Mallon, author of *Children Dreaming*, reports these comments about the nature and function of dreams.

Serapis, the Egyptian god of dreams, was served by dream interpreters known as "the learned men of the magic library."

♒ ♒ Van de Castle

"Dreams are 'pictures in my pillow.'"

—Eva, 4 years

"We dream because we have a problem, then our dreams try to cheer us up."

—Erin, 11 years

"Dreaming helps us get far-back thoughts, which are remote and distant in our minds."

—Rosemary, 13 years

"We dream to rewind our memory."

—Adam, 7 years

"When you want to do something, you have to dream it first so you know how to do it."

—Alvin, 7 years

"We dream so that we don't get fed up while we are asleep."

—Brian, 13 years

Dream Science

Scientific research in the twentieth century was conducted at home in the dreamer's bed and in sleep labs, with CT scans, MRIs and EEG machines. In the mid-1950s, Eugene Aserinsky and Nathaniel Kleitman, at the University of Chicago, observed the connection between Rapid Eye Movement (REM) and dreaming. During sleep, they found that REM alternates with another brain state called Non-Rapid Eye Movement (NREM). As we sleep, the REM phases lengthen, and most dreams occur during these stages.

Sleepers awakened from NREM report thoughts, while most awakened from REM report dreams. As Anthony Stevens puts it in *Private Myths: Dreams and Dreaming,* "NREM reports nonfiction . . . REM reports are fiction."

REM occurs in fetuses in utero, suggesting dream activity.

      Van de Castle

The brain continues to operate while we sleep. During periods of dreaming, the brain stem switches on the cortex to awaken the mind. It switches off the spinal cord to block movement, which is why we do not get up and act out our dreams. Then the brain stem signals the eyes, which causes REM, and stimulates imagery in the visual cortex. REM affects heart rate and blood pressure, and physical arousal usually occurs in this state. REM processes digest, sort, eliminate and integrate the day's experiences, releasing and energizing the psyche so that the sleeper emerges altered. We can go to sleep troubled or possessed by a worry, and when we awaken, there is no problem. We're aware of being unstuck, calm. Our presence to the issue is simpler. We've been naturally pulled back into perspective.

REM sleep facilitates the dream process, though it is not the only state in which dreams occur. Similar cortical activity at the onset of sleep and at awakening can produce dreams characterized by brief thoughts, image fragments, intense emotion and vivid bits of story. Over twenty years ago, I remember popping out of sleep one morning with a fragment of thought crystal clear in my mind: "Clipping whiskers from my father's beard to wear like feathers." I've always thought this ready-made poem was both bizarre and beautiful, an entire relationship condensed into ten words.

On the other hand, I also experienced my most terrifying nightmare in those early minutes of NREM sleep. I encountered Howdy Doody, a woodenheaded marionette from my childhood. He stood suspended in the air before me with his usual freckled grin and cowboy attire. He lifted a gun and pointed it straight at me.

My own screams woke me, and I found myself reaching overhead, pounding on the wall I shared with my neighbors. Within seconds they were at my front door. They came in and searched the house, then took me to their kitchen and gave me a shot of whiskey to calm me down. I was too frightened to be embarrassed and didn't sleep much that night.

That dream image came at a time of huge upheaval in my life. My mother had just died, and I was newly separated from my husband. I had moved into my mother's house and was actually sleeping in her bed when the nightmare occurred. So the scene was set for reminiscence. In my waking mind I was sorting through and reassessing who I was and had been. I was aware of grief over my mother as well as sadness and great guilt over my marriage's ending. Why had my psyche chosen that particular image? What was the experience saying to me?

It took a long time to do anything but run away from that image, but I've thought a lot about it over the years. I'd had my own Howdy Doody doll as a child. He was completely wooden with red painted-on hair, big white teeth, bendable joints and a vacuous, unchanging

> *There is at least one spot in every dream at which it is unplumbable — a navel, as it were, that is its point of contact with the unknown.*
>
> Sigmund Freud

gaze. Every day I'd settle onto the sofa with my whole family of dolls, and we'd watch Howdy and his human sidekick, Buffalo Bob Smith, on television. Squirming children were packed into bleachers called the Peanut Gallery. They cheered and screeched. One day, I got to be a Peanut and made my first television appearance. But Buffalo Bob didn't smile when he talked to us before the show. He didn't seem glad to see us at all and warned us to wave and cheer when we were told to do so.

If you were watching reruns of my childhood, you wouldn't guess that I had never liked Howdy Doody. I certainly never told anyone how disappointing he was to play with. He was so wooden, not responsive like my other dolls that were soft and pliable and could blink and be almost real companions. Santa had brought him, so I had to like him. Even that early, I sorted through my feelings and decided which ones to acknowledge and which to ignore. So, I think about that dream image as the Howdy Doody part of me, the part that doesn't pay attention to my feelings and wishes but just goes along in wooden ways. And I try to remember that the dream framed that habit of woodenness as seriously life threatening, if not to my body, certainly to my soul.

Dreams in Context

I often hear dreamers try to explain last night's dream in terms of events that happened yesterday. I understand that wish to interpret the dream and solve its mystery, but it is never that simple or one-sided. To conceive of where dreams come from and to appreciate them as the holistic events that they are, we need to give equal credence to seemingly opposite elements in ourselves.

That image of you wandering lost in the mall parking lot in the middle of the night is an elegant mix of instinct and intuition, brain waves, body chemicals, emotion, muscle memory and visualization. Body and mind, ego and psyche, left brain and right brain, conscious and unconscious: The physical entwines with the psyche to express an intelligence broader and deeper than our daytime consciousness.

In spending time with dreams, we are listening in on the conversation between our ego, the daytime director of our lives, and our psyche. Psyche is Jung's term for the whole of the personality, including both the conscious and the unconscious. The psyche is the source of life energy that enables continued psychological development. It is like a vast sea on which the ego, like a ship, floats. It's easy to mistake the ego for the psyche. After all, our ego is a fantastic piece of evolution. It focuses and directs, achieves and remembers. It enables our survival in a changing world. Our ego can make us believe we are the center of the universe, which is a very sweet illusion indeed. But it is a limited element of our being. The ego thinks; it operates in a linear, rational manner. Over-attachment to and over-identification with the ego cramps a life, because awake and asleep, the ego doesn't feel, it doesn't imagine and it doesn't dream. Its vision is narrow by comparison to the psyche. Entering our dreams and learning the language spoken there challenges the ego to slow down and use its formidable powers of understanding and action in the service of the psyche.

It is as if consciousness rests upon a self-sustaining and imagining substrate—an inner place or deeper person or ongoing presence—that is simply there even when all our subjectivity, ego and consciousness go into eclipse.

～≈ ～≈ James Hillman

Dreams keep communication open between psyche and ego, and working with dreams brings into consciousness more of the expansiveness that we are. Some people identify the psyche with the experience of God in us. The source of dreams certainly is godlike. Never seen, the psyche generates images organic to the dreamer. These images verify our existence. It is as if someone somewhere were saying, "I know you better than you know yourself. You are a puzzle you will never finish figuring out." Dreams connect us to that larger knowledge and feed our hunger to be known. Our endless quest for love and oneness is, at bottom, a quest for psyche.

I imagine that dreams, then, are a convergence of body and mind, psyche and ego, matter and energy, distilled from the experiences of yesterday and last week, from our childhoods and from the millions of our species' years.

Who Is Dreaming?

Our distance from our dreams is due, in part, to a lack of clarity as to who and what we are. Once we have some notion of what we are, we have a context for our dreams and fantasies.

I often ask my clients what they believe they are and how they are built. They have come in to do some psychotherapy because pain has awakened them to something new in themselves, a persistent sadness or a mysterious anxiety. In a way, symptoms are dreams the mind/body has, metaphorical statements of the system's ennui and indicators about how to proceed. Dreams invite but symptoms insist. And when clients talk about changing something in themselves, I ask what they believe a human is. A body? A mind? What does that mean? How exactly do you work? Are you electromagnetism? An intelligent sack of water? What about the part of you that seems not always under your control? What is that? Who is in control there? And what is it about yourself that you trust? The measurable and provable? The fanciful and idiosyncratic?

My own early education told me in no uncertain terms that I was a body and soul. With many updates on the notion of soul, that definition has continued to make sense to me. Once, I pictured my soul as something I carried around and tried, unsuccessfully, to keep clean of sin. Later, I decided my soul was simply energy. I've settled now in the belief that body and soul are one, inseparable except in the ways we have to talk about them. Body is a denser form of life energy that is my soul. My soul connects me with all of life.

In Hindu tradition, all phenomenal existence is the dream of God or Vishnu.

> Van de Castle

I imagine our lives in the context of transpersonal psychology that tracks the human life cycle from the great unconscious of pre-birth nature through the growing consciousness of early childhood and on to the masteries achieved in adolescence and early adulthood. The functional ego of adulthood learns in the second half of life to find its appropriate place in a consciousness that continues to broaden and deepen. In adulthood, we reconnect the "I," or public persona we've created, with the realities of our own bodies, with others, with the natural environment and with some form of higher power, be it God or Yahweh, Allah, the Life Force, the Universe, or Basic Ground. God goes by many names. As adults, we are combining our intellectual, rational powers with the soulful, imaginal impulse we tasted as children.

So there is another question I ask a new client. What is your spirituality? Not your religion so much as what do you believe in? To imagine where your dreams come from you are also imagining what sort of transcendence you believe in.

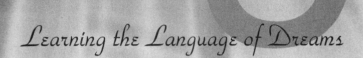

Learning the Language of Dreams

"*Imagination is a transformer that converts invisible material into images the conscious mind can perceive.*"

— Robert Johnson

A Picture Is Worth Thousands of Words

Developed cultures pride themselves on logic, linear thinking, quantitative truth and empirical proofs. The rational becomes equated with what is real, the imaginal with whimsy, superstition and madness. Even in the face of dangerous limitations and catastrophic failures, we cling to the rational for safety and progress and for definitions of who and what we are. We are so deeply entrenched in our culture of logic that it is difficult to even imagine a progressive society that honors its imaginal life equally with its rationality.

Linear thought and logic are accomplishments of the left brain. But before there was a left brain, before there was an alphabet or a language of words as we know it, there were images. Earlier in our evolution, humans experienced the images without the intervention of abstract thought. A growling animal or an empty larder triggered sensations and feelings of danger without making that detour to conceptualize what was happening. Development of the left brain enabled humans to devise more sophisticated protections against "danger" and even to build belief systems with which we distance ourselves from its reality. As linear thought and speech gained sway, the imaginal language lost status until culturally, at least, it is confined to children's play and to sleep.

But the imaginal language continues, carrying the meaning and feeling which are the heart of human experience. Primarily the expression of the older right brain, imagery is the true human vernacular, the hardwired language that transcends time, nationality and geography. It is the stuff dreams are made of, but it also forms the bedrock of our rational waking awareness and permeates our waking life with its energy. Conversely, our deeper imaginal life is stirred and fed by the people, objects and situations we encounter in conscious time. Awake and asleep, we are dreamers, fluent in the language of image. And we can learn a lot about the power of imagery in dreams by looking at our experience of it in waking life.

A typical 75-year-old person has spent 50,000 hours dreaming — that's 2,000 days or 6 years.

                Anthony Stevens

As children, before we possessed the mixed blessing of fully developed brains, the imaginal came naturally to us. The two worlds were not so separate. Monsters stepped out of dreams and hid in closets and under beds until help arrived to chase them away. Imaginary friends shared our toys, and we created kingdoms and clubhouses under sheets or out in fields of high grass. We spoke the imaginal language quite naturally when we said, "I'm Cinderella and you're Prince Charming" or "You be Peter Pan and I'll be Wendy." There was no question then that we could pull out of ourselves these other identities, and for a time, we were Cinderella and Prince Charming and any other imaginal figures that occurred to us.

I first truly understood the power of image and symbol not in connection with dreams but while teaching Language Arts in the '70s to seventh graders. Poised at the brink of adolescence, they seemed hungry for tools to enlarge their worlds, and we were exploring how language generates feelings and pictures while it reveals the vast, undivided nature of reality.

We practiced metaphors:

An apple is sun and rain wrapped in speckled red skin.

My cat has rubber-band legs.

Chocolate rules the world.

That project was a bear.

My room is my fortress.

I taught them to think in similes:

I feel like a slug today.
That teacher is as tough as nails.
His eyes glow like blue fire.

They identified symbols that spoke to them: a red rose for love, the ocean for infinity, a lion as a symbol of bravery. They giggled at the surprise of seeing simple things like apples and homework and love blossom to reveal complex connections with other realities in their worlds. Our work with imagery and metaphor took them deeper into themselves and connected them at their depth with other objects and beings. They were learning the reality of a network of life beyond the rational, mathematical and scientific worlds, and the discovery brought them not just learning but joy.

Imagination was no longer a way to embellish, confabulate or escape the real world. It enlivened language and broadened perception. We began to understand together that imagining and speaking the imaginal language enabled us to see and experience more completely and to go beyond literal meanings. The phrase "His eyes shone like fire" reminded us that eyes do share qualities of fire: the vividness, the liveliness and strength. When they described themselves as tired as a slug, they could experience in their own bodies the moist, slow forward motion of a distant species. They were learning English in those classes, but they were also remembering their original imaginal language and enriching their young lives. That time awakened in me a deep love and new appreciation of the imaginal world. And it set me on a path that eventually led to psychology, where true

Imagination is the primary activity of the soul.

~ ~ Thomas Moore

wellness depends on our ability to live in both worlds and move freely between them.

The Imaginal Life

Even without realizing it, we all participate in the imaginal world quite naturally in our private waking lives. For instance, there are hearts scattered through my home and office. Glass, iron, tin, silver, marble and copper hearts. Some are barely an inch across and the largest measures five inches across. Some are clear, some opaque. You might say I collect hearts, although I don't think of it that way at all and have never described them as a collection. I simply know that I am drawn to them and they remain mysterious companions.

The hearts have both physical and imaginal reality for me. I experience them on both channels. I enjoy their shape, a stylized circle. I'm sure my blood pressure drops at the sight of them. I routinely pick them up, grip their heft and texture, and I enjoy the feel of them. I'll often carry three tiny silver ones in my pocket and listen as they click against each other with solid precise motions.

You could say that the hearts possess me and not the other way around. Their numinosity—the physical and emotional charge they hold for me—is the hallmark of the imaginal. It draws and affects me and takes me beyond rational thinking to the meaning level of my life. Numinous objects have an aliveness, an energy of their own. It is as if every one of my hearts sits in its own glow, as if each is a flame that burns steadily and autonomously. They have the power to transcend time and space and to unite seemingly separate entities. They connect me to my own heart, my own humanity and remind me that there is more to life than the practical and rational. They take me back in time to my father, who struggled with heart disease, and out across distance in the present and future to all I love and hope to be loved by.

We operate in the imaginal and the waking worlds simultaneously, solving problems on both dimensions. In my office, I have a
small, clear glass figure of a whale with Jonah seated inside. He is
raising his hands as if in prayer and frustration with his God. It is an
image that connects me with the timeless human experience I saw
play out in the story of my client Margo.

When Margo gave me the Jonah and the whale figurine, I consulted the Old Testament to
refresh myself on the story.
Jonah was just a regular guy
trying to have a life when
Yahweh told him to go to the
city of Nineveh and warn the
people to mend their ways. This interested Jonah not at all. So
he jumped on a ship and got out of town. He made friends with the
crew and shared his predicament with them so that when a fierce
storm arose, they figured their passenger's troubles with Yahweh
had something to do with it. The storm worsened and then worsened
some more. Jonah told the sailors to throw him overboard and save
themselves. They did and the sea calmed, and Jonah was swallowed
by a whale. There he lived for three days considering his situation
and negotiating with Yahweh. Finally, Jonah agreed to go to
Nineveh, and the whale vomited him onto shore. He completed his
assignment, though he never pretended to have enjoyed it. At the
end of the story, he is still muttering his annoyance at Yahweh.

When Margo came to me, she, too, was deep into a journey she
had not asked for. A bright and likable woman in her late 40s, she
had a family, a good job and ambitions. She'd had an accident that
caused brain damage. She looked normal externally, but inside she
was a jumble of shifting emotions, with little of her previous ability
to focus and make decisions in her life. She was isolated within the

*Symbolic language is language
in which the world outside is a
symbol of the world inside.*

— Erich Fromm

tangle of damaged brain circuits, and she couldn't get out. Life as she had known it was out of her reach.

After much hard work with me and a team of specialists, Margo escaped that awful isolation, reclaimed much of her life and went on to work in the disabilities field. We never spoke of the similarity of her imprisonment within her disability to Jonah's captivity, so I don't know if she consciously saw the parallel. But some resonance occurred that led her to choose that gift.

Our waking lives are filled with such resonances. Think of places and objects and people you have been drawn to. A particular house or car, a color, a tree, a pet, a coin collection, a lover. While they held value in and of themselves, they also resonated with something inside you. It's the feeling people describe when they are falling in love: "I've found my twin." The loved one seems to vibrate at the same frequency, to share the same being. Our choices in the waking world resonate with our inner imaginal world.

We are drawn to things and people who match our inner dramas, which is why getting acquainted with our dream lives is so important. By doing so, we learn what's really going on in us and can live waking life without being swept away by our own mysterious undercurrents. We

Outer circumstances are no substitute for inner experience.

~ ~ C. G. Jung

can then participate consciously in building a life with resonance.

The quality of communication in an image differs from ordinary word communication. For instance, think of the word *candy*. Notice how you feel and what you think about. Now call up a picture of your favorite candy. See it right there in front of you. Notice how you feel now. Notice the difference. The image brings other dimensions of experience, physical and emotional responses engaging not just the mind but the senses also. The word *candy*, while it carries pleasant associations for most of us, is abstract. Those characters, c-a-n-d-y do not innately mean anything. They are a step away from the reality. The image of a fat, dark chocolate truffle with champagne flavoring is not abstract. Focused on the image, I can connect sensually to candy. In our beings, we are more related to image than to word.

The human brain stores data in images. Recall a happy early memory. It will almost certainly be a picture that instantaneously triggers thoughts and feelings. If it is a very strong memory, you might have the sense of actually being there.

Imaginal language differs from everyday speech. It resonates in the whole person and challenges the authority of the logical mind. It carries and evokes emotion, triggers associations and speaks in multiple meanings. It expands rather than specifies.

Returning to candy (remember the truffle?), that image, for me, unfolds into truly sweet memories of being a child and visiting my aunt in the small candy factory where she worked. I associate those visits with the pleasure of being fussed over by all the candy ladies in their white uniforms. My senses engage. I can see the sawdust on worn wooden floorboards. I smell chocolate, hear the whirr of the conveyor belt loaded with its precious cargo. And of course, I can taste the sweet and salty chocolate-covered pretzels I loved so much. The memory is sweet both on the tongue and in the heart and for me associates candy with the security of the womblike candy factory, my awe at the power of my aunt and the other women to create such treasure.

Associations to candy could go on in many directions. Memories of cravings and guilt, of holidays like Valentine's Day and Christmas bring other associations. The image is essentially unplumbable.

We also encounter the imaginal in serious film and drama. Akira Kurosawa's beautiful film *Dreams* illustrates the power of image. Kurosawa used his own dreams in this series of short stories told with minimal dialogue. In each tale, the images create powerful

feeling states. A small boy
sneaks off into lush woods to
spy on the fox's wedding. In
stark black and white, another
story shows a regiment of
ghostly soldiers emerging from

*The word "fantasy" comes from
the Greek "fantasia," which
means to make visible.*

~~ ~~ Webster's New World
College Dictionary

a dark tunnel and reporting to their commander, who is the lone sur-
vivor. Another boy is gifted with one last vision of a long gone peach
orchard. Survivors of a nuclear disaster cling in terror to the dying
land. Each tale begins without preface or explanation, just as dreams
immerse us in another reality. Using outside-of-time rhythms,
Kurosawa draws us in and leaves us imprinted with his imaginal
vision.

Religion and the arts use image intensely and gain their power to
touch and persuade from that numinosity. Imagery also gives music
videos their muscle. The power of the image accounts for the
national addiction to television, regardless of program quality. And
the saying "A picture is worth a thousand words" explains the power
of advertising to capture our imaginations and our money. Beach
vacations, pizza pies, boxer shorts and every other created item
begin imaginally and finish as tangible realities. What advertising
doesn't admit is that you can glean some of the benefits of the beach
vacation by spending time with it here and now in your imagination.
Feel the grit of the sand, the push of the wind, the weight of the sunshine and see that wave breaking. Hear it. Dip your finger in the
foam and taste the salty water. Given our imaginal powers, there is
no reason why that vacation can't start today.

The other imaginal influence in waking life is the cultural mythology, the public dream that subtly but effectively establishes stan-
dards and values for the community. Mythology is found in every
culture and covers the same themes worldwide because it essentially

exists to answer questions about being human. Birth, death, passion, nature, war, wealth, creativity, ambition, loss, generosity, greed — myths show the way through the big experiences and answer our need to make sense out of life. The pop-psychological term "Peter Pan Syndrome" refers to the difficulty of choosing to grow up. The story of Snow White describes the female journey into womanhood. We tell seasonal myths in our observance of major holidays like Christmas, Hanukkah and Kwanzaa.

Many years ago, I told the old myth of Demeter and Persephone to my niece — and myself. As you'll see, the tale, like dreams, tells a story with many meanings.

Brenda and I were driving through a glowing autumn afternoon. She

We've lost certain ancient myths . . . but we're still living myths. We can't ever step outside of a myth.

　　　　James Hillman

was five at the time. We were great friends and had long conversations about many things. I said, "Brenda, do you know why the leaves change color?"

"No," she answered. "Why?"

"I'll tell you. Once upon a time, a queen and a princess lived happily together on the earth where it was always summer. The queen, Demeter, was the Great Mother who took care of the earth and everything that grew on it. She and Persephone played games in the fields and picked flowers and loved being together. Then one day, the princess disappeared and her mother couldn't find her. She searched and searched and finally learned that the princess had been taken to another kingdom underground where she would reign as queen.

"Demeter grieved because she could not go there. Days passed, and she became so sad that she didn't take care of the earth anymore. The flowers wilted and could not bloom again. The grass faded to brown, and the leaves on the trees turned red and yellow and orange as they died. The earth was very still and silent. The sky went gray, and birds no longer sang in the mornings.

"Then a very wise old woman came to the sad queen and said, 'Your majesty, your daughter the princess is all grown-up now. She must rule her own kingdom. She cannot stay with you all the time.' She reminded the queen that the earth needed her attention so that it could live. And she told Demeter that the gods saw her sorrow and offered her this comfort: 'Your daughter will spend half of every year with you and then she will return to her own kingdom.'

"At first the queen was angry. Then she wept. And then she dried her tears and went out into the fields to wait for her daughter. As she waited, she sang to the earth and the sky. Slowly the flowers stretched out of their sleep. The grass greened and its fragrance woke the birds. As the old woman had promised, the princess came home to her mother. For six months they walked in the fields and laughed together and shared many secrets. When the time came for Persephone to leave, Demeter's sadness again spilled over the earth and all the green faded away. The trees glowed red and yellow. Winter followed. And this happened every year. And that is why the leaves change colors.

"Do you like that story, Brenda?"

Without taking her eyes off the brilliant leaves, she said, "Tell me again, Aunt Emma."

That myth personified the seasonal shift and that was my conscious reason for telling Brenda the story. But, like dreams, this old myth told other stories, notably one of separation and reunion. I knew that Brenda and her family would be moving to Europe within the year and that she would finish her growing up there. At the time, I didn't realize the parallel between the myth and our situation, but it gave me a model of how big changes can happen without destroying connection. The myth soothed my own sadness at the coming separation and helped me refocus on the new pattern our relationship would take. And the story came true for us. Our relationship found new rhythms, and now as reliably as seasons change, Brenda appears at my door for visits.

Public dreams express themselves in many ways. Epic tales like *Star Wars* and *Harry Potter* give a contemporary face to good and evil. Economic myths dictate what is enough and who has a right to have it. Spiritual mythology shapes our ideas of God and of who has access to the Divine. Social mythology explains how we are with each other, who's on top, who belongs and who doesn't. It illustrates what relationships should look like and says who is allowed to partner with whom.

> *Symbols have intrinsic meanings and they carry emotion as well as meaning.*
>
> Edward Whitmont

Thanks to technology, even before we leave the house in the morning, we've been exposed to an array of mythology dispensed by TV, radio and newspapers and tweaked by endless products in bathrooms and kitchens, each of which carries a message and a promise. The world is eager to supply us with mythologies that tell us who we are. Without the anchor of our own dream lives and the personal mythologies that begin there, we run the risk of living someone else's life.

Night Dreams

In all these ways, the imaginal interweaves with our waking lives. But when we go to sleep, we plunge fully into its mystery. Using the people, places and things of waking life, the psyche paints pictures and tells stories. Meanings associate out into a network of connections we had never considered before. Dreams occur and return. They feel no obligation to get to the point. They blend issue and emotion into an image that connects past and future, inside and outside us, the world and our physical selves, consciousness and the unconscious. A dream house may resonate with experiences of nurturing from early in my life or with my protective attitude toward my body or my wish for safety and security. Feelings or the absence of feeling reveal more information than our waking minds can grasp. These images introduce new themes and reframe problems. The imaginal impulse models innate aliveness, the moving, flexible nature of our own being with its unlearned, innate wisdom. It disrupts stagnation and encourages the natural processes of change.

Imaginal language is witty and uses puns and word play. It is precise at the same time that it is lush and dense. Like mythology, it can be read from many angles and at different points in a life; it can be read for different meanings. It is *the* organic art form. It affirms the richness of existence in a way that the utilitarian tongue of every day does not. C. G. Jung called it the voice of nature itself.

Dreams use the imaginal to personify impersonal reality: A crying child may represent sadness, or a lion tearing at its prey, aggression. Images are not literal but can mean any number of things depending on the context of the dream and the unique circumstances of the dreamer. While it is a tree, a tree is also a home, a lonely mourner or a protector. A kitchen could be a science lab or a magician's den, a prison or a warm feathered nest. A bed may imply sexuality or refuge or loneliness. And a toilet can represent both loss and messiness and fruitfulness and transformation. We read dreams in their many meanings and come closer to understanding the undividedness of life.

My own dreams and those of my clients speak the imaginal language:

"I am in a class and we are flying like a flock of large, strong birds over a stand of trees."

"I am a glittering silver woman sitting on a swing."

"My ceiling-to-floor curtains are gauzy maps of the world."

"I am left alone in the woods, and I am feeling like an abandoned child."

"My lover and I watch each other from grassy hilltops, and suddenly, the hills begin to drift farther away from each other."

"My neighborhood is a war zone. All I own is a large armored truck."

These dream fragments brim with inferences and feelings unique to the world of each dreamer. Some images are fantastic, like the drifting hilltops. Others, like the war zone scene, happen in the external world every day. Dream language is like code, knowable only to the dreamer, who must intuit the message's meaning with his own instincts.

Some dreams address the great themes of life. Jung called these basic themes archetypes. They are the species' imperatives, psychic structures and natural inclinations, such as motherhood, fatherhood, the hero, the warrior, the lover, the healer and the old wise person. They are etched into our psyches, and we play out our unique renditions of the archetypes in waking behaviors and in dreams.

Each of us is a full cast of archetypal impulses. As Anthony Stevens says in *Private Myths: Dreams and Dreaming*, "No one is alone. Everyone is a crowd." The emergence of unfamiliar and unappealing aspects of ourselves surprises and dismays us. We prefer to believe that we are a solid unity and that this unity is basically good. We value steadiness to the point of robotlike efficiency. But our dreams decimate those visions and present us to ourselves as fluid, complex and changeable like any other part of nature. It can be a shock to witness that variety within ourselves. We'd like to avoid meeting our darker aspects, like the murderer or the self-absorbed child. But that internal chorus of good and bad, innocent and treacherous, is normal reality.

Less than one percent of dreams have the written word in them.

Van de Castle

The basic truth about archetypes is that if you don't see them coming, they can knock you off your feet. They carry huge emotional charges, which we experience as the power of love or hate or aggression. Who hasn't found himself totally gripped by the experience of falling in love, or hating someone? Archetypes are potentials and innately do not have limits. It's up to us to modulate their power, and dreams help integrate that power into conscious life by introducing it in a story.

Here's an archetypal dream.

Sophie was at home. The front door opened and in came an oddly dressed man in colors and patterns that didn't match. She wasn't exactly afraid of him, more unnerved and annoyed that he walked right in as if he were familiar with her home. He climbed the stairs, looked around, turned and came down again. There was something impish about him. She was very unhappy about his being in the house.

Just a snippet of dream, wordless and plotless. But now, 15 years later, Sophie's visitor is still with her and informing one of the primary themes of her adulthood. She is acquainted with the jester. She still has mixed feelings about him. She still prefers that he would have barged into someone else's house. But when she returns for a few sessions every now and then, and we sort through her issues, she will regularly look at me across the coffee table, laugh and say, "There's the jester again!"

When Sophie first met the jester in that tiny "Big Dream," her life had just been disrupted when her husband of twenty-some years was blinded in an automobile accident. He had been a successful, dynamic architect, and the injury threw him into a depression from which he'd never quite recovered. He was no longer her rock and her provider, and plans they'd made for their future crumbled.

Sophie's role shifted from partner to caretaker, cheerleader and comforter. But as months passed and her husband's withdrawal hardened, she found herself in a morass of rage and mourning and loneliness. One of Sophie's core beliefs had been that staying alert in the world would keep misfortune away.

As she told her story, I was struck by the shock that still echoed through the words. "This isn't my life anymore. I don't know whose it is! I want my own life back. I want Peter the way he was. He's been ruined—we're both ruined." Sophie stormed and wept, horrified by their bad fortune and also by her reaction. "I'm so angry at Peter for having the accident, and for just giving up. Mostly for that. Giving up. At the same time, I'm ashamed of my anger and impatience. He's a good man; we've had a good life. And here I am resenting him for something that wasn't his fault. I don't know if I can do this. I don't know if I can stay with him."

Perhaps we might say he [the fool] represents a redemptive factor within ourselves that urges us on towards individuation.

≈ ≈ Sallie Nichols

Nothing in Sophie's past had prepared her for this turn of events. Her growing-up years had been unremarkable, just the usual developmental challenges, the usual experiences of conflicts, money problems, disappointments. Now, Sophie felt unsafe, threatened by ill fortune bigger than she was. Then she dreamed of that strange man walking into her house.

It was the clothes that gave him away. As Sophie talked about her dream, certain details began to catch my attention. She was not afraid of the man, just annoyed. He was strangely dressed "in colors and patterns that didn't match." And "there was something impish about him." I told Sophie about the traditional figure of the jester. In fairy tale, myth and literature, he goes by many names—the fool, the trickster, the joker. He is one of the basic archetypes woven into the psyche of all humans. The jester is unflappable. He knows he is a fool and he knows how to roll with the punches. He destroys illusion and speaks the unvarnished truth.

He is the restless Puck in *A Midsummer Night's Dream,* playing tricks on lovesick humans. And he is a company of clowns balancing the danger and tension created by roaring lions at the circus. He is the stand-up comedian commenting on the follies of politicians. He is the wanderer of the Tarot who acts "by insight rather than eyesight" according to Sallie Nichols' description in *Jung and Tarot: An Archetypal Journey.* He is the wild card that appears and alters the fortunes of gamblers. He stepped into Sophie's life when everything was upside down. In modern motley, he ignored the convention of knocking and being received. He sized up the situation and made himself at home. He brought confirmation that the unexpected and the senseless happen. Then life goes on with its indiscriminate vitality.

The power of the archetype began to work on her as I described the jester. Sophie's mood changed. Her annoyance with the intruder softened a bit, and she was drawn into the vast company of humans who have suffered a visit from Fate. She recognized in her situation and in her dream that she was not isolated and not a freak of nature because bad luck had come her way. The visit of the jester validated her experience and gave it dignity. In a reluctant alliance with the jester, she found firm ground to begin to deal with her lot.

It is not I who create myself, rather I happen to myself.

~ ~ C. G. Jung

His appearance reminded Sophie of what she knew under her rage and sadness: Life happens. It's unpredictable and unfair. Wisdom, survival and transcendence come with seeing and acknowledging things as they are.

Our dreams sketch out our own private mythology in which good and evil, the sublime and the ridiculous play out the themes of our lives. Sophie had dreamed of an encounter with Fate. Another woman, six months pregnant, dreams of deep-sea diving and finds exotic sea creatures. The images in her dream—salt water, water creatures—add up to her own fertility myth and place her waking experience into a larger context. A young man works on an old house in a long series of dreams. Changes in the house tell the story of his own transformation. During a period of preoccupation with her aging, an old woman dreams of being lost in a city, without subway fare and in the company of a lion. Her dream mythologizes her current challenges. The private mythologies of our dreams tell us about our humanity and provide landmarks in our passage through life. They round out our idea of who we are and sometimes they correct it. They anchor us so that we can participate in the culture's public mythology without losing ourselves.

Dreamwork Practice

Come back with me to my Neanderthal dream as I work with it. I've found that naming dreams is another way to get inside them, and I've decided to call this one, ironically, "A Day at the Beach." I toyed with titles for a few days and this is the first one that has clicked with me. It feels right in my gut and makes me chuckle. A title, like an image, has the power to compress and crystallize information about the dream. In this case, it suggests a tongue-in-cheek quality to the dream. Usually I think of a day at the beach as sunshine, blue sky, sparkling water and nothing to do. Here it is all black and white and gray, and the water is not visible. The man does seem to be doing nothing, but in a very conscious deliberate way. For most of us, days at the beach are special. They're few and far between, relatively speaking. The scale of that environment breaks us out of our daily trance. That seems to be true here, too, but this scene is a very long way from our usual idea of a day at the beach. It offers a different view of what renewal and refreshment look like. It expands my beach ideas of idleness, effortlessness and timelessness.

Let's sit on the sand a little ways off from the man where we can take in the whole scene. The important thing is to play and wonder. Much like a reporter gathers information by answering the basic questions *who? what? where? when?* and *how?*, we can begin by gathering basic information.

Who is here? What are they like?

What is happening?

Where am I? What do I see as I look around?

When is this happening?

How do I feel? What do others seem to be feeling?

This is what I find as I sit in the dream. I see that this is a very simple scene. There is none of the paraphernalia we usually cart to the beach. The weather is overcast, and there's no way to know what time it is. This is a place outside of time. It has a faraway feeling. I see the huge boulders between us and the sea. I know there is a cave behind me to the right, and in the center of this clearing is the man crouched next to lines in the sand.

The scene is naturally enclosed by boulders on three sides. It is stripped down and unadorned, but even in black and white, it looks vital. The enclosure of the scene feels soothing to me, and the Spartan look of it makes me a little anxious.

The man remains motionless and focused. He seems to be meditating, which is a way of coming to an understanding without thinking. He is the antithesis of boredom. He is as unencumbered as the beach is. He is new in a way; the newness comes from his ability to be present. His age in years doesn't matter.

I am drawn down the long rail-like indentations in the sand and can imagine following them for miles and miles. I wonder if the man can actually see far places along the tracks. The tracks are like time, like linear progress. Here we watch it but are not part of it. Here the linear and the timeless meet, material and mental, the iron in the balls and the lightness of attention. Phrases like "walk the line" and "cross the line" occur to me.

As far as senses go, I can feel the coarse, damp sand and the still, cool air. I don't hear any sounds; the ocean must be very calm today. I see the lines in the sand, the black round balls, the huge black boulders and the gray sky.

I am very interested in the small, heavy balls and am reminded of the weights in my father's fishing tackle box. I can imagine the feel of one in the palm of my hand. Solid. Surprising in its density. I like that sensation. It's like concentrated presence. Like holding it could insure my own undivided presence.

> *I never lost the sense that where my dreams come from is where I come from.*
>
> ❧ ❧ Elizabeth Rose Campbell

This dream feels like a beginning, the first scene of a new script. It reminds me of a poem I wrote ten years ago.

Waking Instructions
Crawl ashore
to the damp beginning of day.
Forget before and after.
Allow yourself
to be spelled differently.
It will feel like falling.
It has waiting attached.

Every dream comes with "waiting attached." We have to wait for the daytime mind to settle, wait for the images to reveal their meanings, wait to feel that sense of knowing in our guts. We are so used to left-brained thinking that this waiting, this hanging out with the unknown can feel quite unproductive. But in this waiting, we are crossing the line into our other way of knowing. It is an organic process, as natural as a sandy beach turning into ocean.

Let's step out of the dream now. I stand back and observe how the encounter with the scene has affected me. Your own experience of the dream will differ from mine. I'm not ready to say what the dream means, but I can feel the reality of it more strongly now. The stillness of the scene contrasts so sharply with my usual overbusy routine. I'm wondering about things I miss or take for granted in my day: the birds at the feeder outside my window, the feel of my body, the sun on my face, the quality of a friend's voice, the taste of an apple.

More questions occur to me. How do I do in situations that are stripped down, simple, elemental? Actually, there aren't that many. I carry things to do and things to think about wherever I go. Like everyone else, I multitask and take pride in doing it well. What if I made regular time for stillness? How would that change me?

I find I am curious and pleased to have this new place as part of my awareness. I look forward to returning there. The questions that arise bring feelings of interest, excitement, uneasiness. I want to go out to the garage and find that old tackle box and hold a weight in the palm of my hand. Of course, I wonder if I'm doing this right, but I let that thought pass.

Notice how being in this dream has affected you emotionally and physically. Are new questions occurring to you? Do the dream's images point you to associations in your own life? You can practice on this dream or apply similar questions to a dream of your own.

The years when I was pursuing my inner images were the most important in my life—in them everything essential was decided.

C. G. Jung

I have begun to claim the substance of this dream for my conscious life. I can feel the tickle of interest that comes with having something new and mysterious. I can feel the reality of the dream, not as something that is made-up and frivolous but as a collection of images and experience that take up energy and space in my consciousness. I am starting to believe in it. That's enough, more than enough, for now.

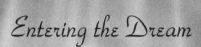

Entering the Dream

"... our dreams represent our primordial habitat, our last wilderness, and we must protect them with as much fervor as the rain forests, the ozone layer, the elephant and the whale."

—Robert Johnson

Taming Obstacles

A story in Greek mythology tells about a bereaved widower named Orpheus who goes to the underworld in search of his wife, Euridyce. It is a bold act. The dim and shadowy underworld does not welcome the living. But Orpheus is bereft without Euridyce, so he makes the descent. At the gate, Orpheus encounters the terrible watchdog, Cerberus. The beast snarls and lunges to strike. And against all logic, Orpheus begins to strum his lute. Cerberus calms and turns gentle. He admits Orpheus to the castle where he will be reunited with Euridyce.

When we dream, we, too, descend to an underworld. We leave consciousness for the unknowable unconscious. Familiar ways of being disappear. We encounter lost parts of ourselves, some beloved, some feared and some we've never met. When we revisit and work with our dreams, we enter that realm again, and if, like Orpheus, we are to be successful, we must enter dreams on their own terms.

Every dreamer faces obstacles at the dream's threshold. Much of what threatens our entrance reflects beliefs and concerns we've brought from the daytime world. Here's an example.

> *. . . we see our devils, our shadow, in others. The shadow, or at least its dark side, is composed of . . . all those things about ourselves we are not proud of and regularly seek to hide from others."*
>
> ᐁ ᐁ Daryl Sharp

A certain high profile, millionaire building mogul who is definitely not one of my favorite famous people, made a guest appearance in one of my dreams recently. As I related the dream to a friend, I assured him that I hadn't meant to dream about this man and that he certainly wasn't someone I admired. I find my icons in literature, psychology, philosophy and the arts—proving, if only in my own mind, what a superior person I am. The dream made me uncomfortable, and I needed to disown my connection to the mogul and all he represented for me. Surely, a freak electromagnetic surge in the universe had caused me to dream someone else's dream. Wrong images, wrong dream. That couldn't be about me.

My reaction illustrates the nearly universal proclivity of dreamers to disown dreams. We preface or end the telling of a dream with a disclaimer like "I had a really weird dream" or "This is so crazy" or "This makes no sense." We treat dreams like deranged and delinquent adolescents, and while we have to give them room and board, we certainly aren't eager to be seen with them in public. We don't want to be held responsible for what they say and do.

We fear dreams will misrepresent us, expose secrets, reveal that we are strange, inferior, evil or crazy. They're all human worries, and they bar our entrance to our own imaginal world as surely as the hostile Cerberus guarded the iron gate of the underworld.

Dreams don't spin their messages. Niceties disappear in REM sleep. All those polite conventions we use to grease the great wheels of social interaction evaporate. Dreams reveal our shadowy, messy underside and our unlived brilliance. The more rigid and homogenous our persona in the daytime world, the more outrageously will the imaginal world insist on balance with revelations of our darker secrets.

For instance, a soft-spoken, gentle young man reports dreams of himself in barroom brawls and street fights. An elegant older woman sees herself as an infant peeing on an important man. A successful salesman dreams of poverty. Dreams show aspects of our situations and personalities that may be quite foreign and others that may be familiar but nothing to be proud of. We may see ourselves in dreams as selfish, irresponsible, dull-witted or cowardly. Or the dream may show us in the midst of fabulous beauty and good fortune. "Not me," we say to ourselves. But it is me.

We appear in our own dreams as heroes and cowards, conspirators, fools, seducers and seduced. I can sympathize when dreamers worry that whole other personalities are brewing in there, waiting for a little attention to take over. They worry that the prostitute, Darth Vader, a shoplifter, a toddler in a tantrum or a bag lady who appears in dreams are aspects of themselves that will turn their daytime worlds upside down. But those characters are only looking for a little daylight and room to stretch. They're not coming to take over. They just want a place at the table.

> *Realization of the shadow is inhibited by the persona, the ideal image we have of ourselves . . . The persona aims at perfection. The shadow reminds us we are human.*
>
> — Daryl Sharp

None of us is only what our daily façade advertises. We each are multitudes. Our identities are more rich and broad than we know. Putting ethics aside for the moment, not evaluating on the basis of right and wrong, female and male, it is as if we are built to experience all 360 degrees of life, to choose from among many possibilities of who we will be moment to moment. We each are capable of the best and the worst, and dreams that parade the worst can be challenging to work with.

On the other hand, dreams are a mercy because they release us from the constraints of the daytime persona with its logical, linear rules. The more familiar we are with the cast of characters we ferry through life, the richer our existence will be and the less likely that any part will overwhelm or surprise us.

Yes, that's just the opposite of what you've been told. You're much less likely to cheat on your taxes if you are in touch with that aspect of yourself that wants something for nothing. Ethical behavior is a choice from among many options. If you prefer to pretend that the wish to get something for nothing isn't within you, your psyche will probably deliver a dream to prove it is. Dreams tell the story of our vast possibilities.

Even our daytime solidity is an illusion. Quantum science has shown that at a subatomic level, we are spacious and extremely variable, more energy than matter. Though we and all the objects in our world appear solid, at the most basic level all are in continuous change. What was true in the past minute does not predict reality in this minute or the next. Possibility is the norm and sameness the aberration. The imaginal world consists of that same abundance.

For most of us, though, the spell of the imaginal is broken each morning. We open our eyes and fall under another spell. In the tumbling and aggressive forward motion of our days, efficiency and predictability rule. Our world is so dumbed down and honed to convenience that dreams seem obscure by comparison. We have lives to live, groceries to pick up, children to ferry around, lawns to mow, dogs to walk. Not to mention jobs to do and relationships to cultivate. Not one of those situations is particularly interested in our complexity. Life on the clock proceeds automatically as long as we keep all but the voice of the ego under wraps. Unfortunately, Cerberus eats egos for mid-morning snacks.

Our immersion in the rational world devours the imaginal. It is so much easier to go to the bookstore and buy a dream dictionary than it is to sit quietly and receptively in the presence of last night's dream and wait for understanding to develop. Our spectacular technologies have brought us control and speed. We have come to accept the artificial and static in exchange for promises of reliability, consistency and safety. Through the Internet, we've gained access to almost infinite sources of prepared information. It's easy to get lost in all that thought and forget that we and our dreams are part of nature in a way that information is not. In that state of mind, we can miss opportunities for the immeasurable and the original. We're left running in rational circles; boundaries harden and the dream world becomes less accessible. As living, breathing bits of nature, we need the fresh food of dreams to survive and thrive. And there is an endless supply available.

The unconscious and its vital symbolic life are to our rational consciousness as the sea is to a tiny sailboat. Everything that we believe, accomplish, create and experience rides on that vast sea and draws life from its vitality. Our rational faculties can't do the job alone.

And finally, we are kept from entering our dreams by that nagging complaint that they are just too weird. In our dreams, we fly, lose our teeth, find ourselves in two places at once and talk to others who are two people at once, find rooms in our houses we didn't know were there, talk with animals, travel through underground labyrinths, speak with the dead, foresee the future, make love with strangers, move forward and backward in time, take lives and save them. Even so, the strangeness of dreams can't compete with the bizarre happenings of waking life we witness and participate in. Consider this: On television this week, you can probably see people eating worms and exposing their darkest secrets to millions of viewers, being possessed by devils, talking with spirits, and killing their loved ones. The news is full of world leaders saying the sky is yellow, or up is down, with no consequences.

Whatever strangeness exists in our waking lives is there because we've chosen it or because it at least lies within what the culture says is normal. But the strangeness of dreams comes by a different authority—our own unconscious. It is not sanctioned by any outer power, not even the waking ego. And there's the rub. In our dream lives, we have the sense that our "I" isn't in control. There is no narrow egotistical agenda here. While we are curled in sleep, our own basic nature is telling us stories, showing us to ourselves from the deep nature point of view. Dreams can be awesome experiences, and religions have been founded to buffer exactly that direct powerful contact with nature.

Entering the Dream

We step inside our dreams with one agenda: to search and find, as Orpheus did, what we need for our very deepest well-being. We enter with attentiveness, intuition, patience and creativity. We allow ourselves, at first, not to know what this dream is about.

The first step is to recall the dream in as much detail as possible. It is as if we emerge from sleep connected to our dreams by gossamer threads that dissolve at the slightest disturbance. Even ordinary movements can erase the memory. You can increase your dream recall by getting in the habit of checking as soon as you are conscious if you've dreamed, even before you open your eyes or move your head. Those moments of awakening are a fertile threshold, and it can pay to linger there, simultaneously asleep and awake. Allow it to be a gentle passage—this is not the time for a blast of talk radio. Catch whatever wisps of image, emotion and language you've brought into the day. Observe and note whatever comes to you, whether it makes sense or not. Review the dream, write it down or speak it into a tape recorder before rising.

Fantasy-images provide the basis of consciousness . . . Becoming conscious would now mean becoming aware of fantasies and the recognition of them everywhere and not merely in a "fantasy world" separate from "reality."

James Hillman

This waking ritual cultivates an openness, a state of mind that appreciates the reality of both worlds. It bridges our passage into the day world. And taking time to remember and record dreams actually increases the likelihood that we will recall still more dreams tomorrow.

Since there aren't many mornings when we can lie abed and travel back into fresh dreams, notes preserve the images until we can make time for reflection. Even in a busy world, the important things get done. Setting aside a regular time and place to work with dreams adds depth and texture to life and increases accessibility to the imaginal. That quiet room or comfortable chair where you do dream work becomes like another threshold between the worlds. With practice, settling into that spot will happen more seamlessly.

Stumbling into the light of morning, or from an afternoon nap into the lit house at suppertime, we are realized as fragile temporary beings. Why should our waking be more real than the just-past dreaming?

Richard Grossinger

Begin by dropping out of your mind's chatter, settle down into your body. Take some calming breaths. If it helps you focus, put on music or light a candle—anything that demarcates this time and effort from the day's concerns, anything that helps you shift out of your thoughts into your imagination.

I can illustrate that shift by describing an experience I had recently. I sat down to watch the film *Baraka,* an hour-and-a-half-long montage of humans in their environments around the world. To my surprise, the film had no overt plot and no narrative. It was like a dream: subtle, vital, full of slowly emerging patterns. Now we are in a rainforest, now on a New York City street, now at a Buddhist temple in Bangkok, and now at an industrial chicken farm some-where in the middle of America. People speak foreign languages, yet we know what they mean.

At the beginning, I was impatient for a plot. My mind buzzed. I wanted a story with a beginning, middle and end. It had been a long day and I wanted someone to tell me what it was all about. I wanted to be organized and entertained, and I didn't want to work at it. But as time passed, the rhythm and the subtle thematic connections slowed and quieted me, and I sank into the flow of images. In a much more receptive way, I let the images touch me. The film shifted me from "thinking about" to "connecting with." It wasn't tiring. All I had to do was get out of my way and allow myself to be drawn into the images. And that's what needs to happen when we enter our dreams.

Let's practice with a dream from a female client in her 20s:

> *My mother and I are seated on a large rock in the center of a grouping of boulders.*
>
> *We are looking down into the space between the boulders at a Gerber daisy. There is a sheet of plexiglass over it. I'm frustrated because she is showing me a flower confined under plastic. That's not where flowers belong.*

As if it were your own dream, use your imagination to settle on the next rock over from the dream figures and observe what's going on. Slow yourself down and look around. Don't worry that you don't know the details of the dream, such as what the women looked like or what their relationship in waking life is like.

Fill in the details with your imagination. What can you see? No need to draw conclusions; simply observe. Look at the mother and daughter. What expressions are on their faces? How have they arranged themselves on the rocks? Imagine the larger scene. What are the colors and objects within sight? Is the scene still or is there movement? What are the sounds and scents of the place? What are the textures around you? What is the mood in the scene? What emotions do you sense in the mother and the daughter? What is the most striking aspect of the dream? What jumps out at you? How do you feel as a visitor to the scene?

Dreams typically reflect one's daily concerns and customary lifestyle. A departure from conventional behavior in your dreams may anticipate the possibility of a new direction in your waking life.

Stanley Krippner
& Joseph Dillard

Don't ask what the dream means. Simply be in the scene. Using all your senses, take it in. Allow the scene to affect you.

Accept what you are imagining about the women. I'm suggesting that you own what your imagination is telling you. Practice trusting your intuition and imagination. When doubts or self-criticism arise, notice them and let them pass.

If you have difficulty visualizing the dream, simply visit the story and notice what you notice in the way that it comes to you: the mood of the scene, their voices, the physical feel of the rocks or the scents of the place. If you are receptive, the dream will most probably open itself to you in some way. For now, all you have to do is find the imaginal channel that will take you into the scene.

This dream presents a very basic human experience: an encounter between parent and child, more specifically, between mother and daughter. By imagining the dream images, you've peopled this archetypal situation with your own history, experiences, perceptions and values. If you'll review what you've seen, you'll find information about yourself as parent and/or child. Here's how it went for my client Grace.

Grace felt agitated as she began talking about her dream. She was focused on the flower and the frustration of not being able to get to it. She said she liked Gerber daisies and felt her mother was to blame for the plexiglass. The scene reflected her beliefs that her mother's pessimism and caution had narrowed her—Grace's—own world. Theirs had been a tense relationship, marked more by their differences than their similarities. It was as if her mother had always existed behind a wall of plexiglass. What surprised Grace most was the frantic feel of her dream self, who was ruminating about how flowers should not be penned in like the daisy in her dream. She wondered why her mother was always so worried and distant. She also noticed there had been no dialogue between them.

I encouraged her to wander around in the scene, and when she did she noticed details she had missed the first time. During dream work, it's not unusual to discover details that were missed when initially telling the dream. Grace recalled that there was bird song and the distant sound of the ocean. It was a sunny day, not too hot and without a noticeable breeze. The boulders were broad and solid and smooth under her hands. She saw her dream-self looking uncomfortable and restless. Her mother, on the other hand, was calm and smiling. This surprised Grace. I asked her to imagine sitting with them. She did and reported that the mother was quite calm, engaged and gentle. This was different from what she had expected. As we talked, she felt her resentment at the mother figure melting away. It dawned on her that the mother was showing the daughter something she had no words for, a life growing beautifully among boulders, taken special care of and then shared.

Grace left the dream scene quite rattled. Her struggles with her mother had been a significant part of our work together, but this dream had taken us down a different path. She'd seen the caring aspect of her mother, who, against significant odds, had made a good life for herself and her family. Her mother's courage and hope were something like the Gerber daisy; still vital, though her life had been rocky. Grace could see the gift the dream-mother was offering. It was the beginning of my client's release from the resentment and disappointment that she had thought were her only inheritance.

The meaning of the dream emerges from the experience of the dream. Grace had gone back into the scene, looked with new eyes at the images and gathered information. The images touched her and triggered changes in her feelings and opinions. Though her mother had been dead for many years, Grace's ongoing internal relationship with her had developed beyond their old stalemate.

The dream doesn't ask us to change; it changes us.

~ ~ Richard Grossinger

Like all good metaphors, dreams are rich in meaning. They can be viewed from many angles. This time it was the daisy that riveted Grace's attention. At another time, it could be the boulders or her mother's expression or the plexiglass itself or something about her dream self. Your own visit to the dream may have felt very different from Grace's experience, and it, like hers, could change with circumstances in your waking life or your particular needs at another time. A dream is like a jewel with many facets. Its many meanings reflect the complexity of our natures, the constant reconfigurations of energy and experience that add up to who we are. Nothing about us is solid. Nothing is final. The psyche is a process of becoming, a constant expansion of consciousness. In this case, the dream work has broadened Grace's experience of being a daughter to include the ability to receive from a deeply caring mother.

Here's another dream, this one from a 35-year-old woman:

I was late for a flight and could not find the correct airport. I was on a winding mountain road, driving a rather beat-up Volkswagen Rabbit convertible. I had a girlfriend with me in the passenger's seat, and I think it was Kcee with blonde hair, not her current red hair. We stopped at an airport that we knew was not the correct one and asked a bearded man how much farther to the next airport. He told us, "Go left, go left and go left. Three lefts, a mile apart from one another, and you will be there." We got back in the car and no sooner had we started but we pulled over again to put the top up. We were now on a busy San Francisco residential street in the Castro. We took a large, old-fashioned, heavy, metal-type baby carriage out of the backseat so that we could put the top up. We folded up the baby carriage and put it inside a stranger's garage that happened to have one of its black barn-style doors open. As we stepped back from the house, a man appeared in the window above and tapped on the glass. He pointed to a large black bear coming up the sidewalk. I was not afraid of it, really, no more afraid than I would be of an unfamiliar dog. Kcee grabbed some sort of meat from our cooler and threw it to the bear. The bear ate the meat and hopped into the back seat of the car. Of course, we were still unable to put the top up. I figured I had missed my flight, but we began to drive anyway. . . . Then we were suddenly in an ice rink. Wearing rented plastic ice skates, I could skate remarkably well.

Step into this dream for another exercise in imagination. If the bear disturbs you, imagine yourself invisible to the bear. Or place a glass wall between you and the bear. And once again, draw no conclusions. Simply observe. Check your senses: What do you see, hear, feel and smell? To whom or what are you drawn? If you could join the action, how would you do that? What emotions does this dream trigger in you? There are no wrong answers to any of these questions. You are using your imaginal senses. Your reaction will be unique.

You can go on to note your associations to aspects of the dream. Who or what in the dream reminds you of aspects of your own life? Maybe the car triggers memories. Or perhaps being late for flights or carrying a baby carriage in the car strikes you with a sense of familiarity. In associating to your own life, you are connecting the dots between the visible and imaginal and beginning to discover the symbolic echoes of ordinary moments in your waking life.

This dream connected Lil with her present and her past. Responding to the dream, she recounted adolescent memories of the Castro. She'd had to travel through there every day on her way to high school. It was the '70s. She'd loved exploring the head shops and felt completely at home in the freedom and adventure of the place. Boundaries blurred in the Castro and imagination and innovation reigned. Twenty-five years later, her voice brimmed over with the joy of that time.

The bear has served as a sacred symbol to many ancient cultures . . . Neanderthals constructed shrines or altars to the Master Bear and buried bear skulls and bones alongside their own. Ancient shamans in North America, Iceland, Finland, Siberia, and Japan carved, engraved, painted, or otherwise depicted the bear as a sacred animal. The bear has both solar and lunar aspects in Scandinavian and Teutonic traditions, being sacred to the masculine sky god Thor . . . as well as to the lunar goddesses of the water.

— Elizabeth Caspari

The dream seemed to point out to her that the intelligent, free-spirited aspect of Lil found herself at age 35 driving in circles—"Go left, go left and go left." She was living in the diligent, serious and conscientious part of herself, trying to conform to schedules and the requirements of her career and relationships. But she was behind schedule and somewhat lost. Lil found in the dream a capsulated version of one of the core conflicts of her life: the struggle between her creative, adventurous self and her more practical, responsible self.

The final scene gave her hope that some solution was possible, and she took great comfort in it. Skating had been her passion as a child. She recalled the figure eights, the weaving motion that is the symbol of infinity and wholeness. "Better than making endless left turns in a ratty VW Rabbit," she said.

I am always happy to work on animal dreams. They have a vitality and wit I enjoy. They bring instinct and raw nature into our lives. The Jungian analyst Marie-Louise von Franz writes that one truth she's found in her study of fairy tales is that those individuals whom animals help always win out. The same is true of encounters with animals in dreams.

Imagining

When you feel drawn to a character or an object in a dream, you can open a dialogue with it. We call that process active imagination, and remember, we're talking about imagination here as a valid way of connecting with the dream world. Jungian analyst Robert Bosnak calls it "a discipline of the imagination." He writes, "In active imagination, you don't have the feeling of unreality; it is rather as if you participate in two equally true realities simultaneously: the world that is actively imagined *and* the world in which you know that you are involved in active imagination." This exercise gives you the opportunity to discover more about figures in the dream. You can interact, ask questions and listen as your questions are answered.

> *Writing is for many the most satisfying form of active imagination. You have a dialogue in what's going on inside. You conjure up an image of what you're feeling, personify it and talk to it, then you listen to what it says back. You write this down to make it real, to give it substance. That's the difference between active imagination and a daydream.*
>
> — Daryl Sharp

Lil wanted to revisit her dream bear. I asked her beforehand to list questions she'd like to ask him. She made herself comfortable where she wouldn't be disturbed, took a few slow, deep breaths to quiet her mind and relax her body. She returned to the scene on the residential street. Her friend has just thrown the bear a piece of meat that he has eaten.

This is how the active imagination went. The sentences in parentheses are Lil's comments as the experience happened.

Lil: Are you still hungry?
Bear: I'm good. Let's roll.

(He's very laid-back and cool, the way I'd like to be. Very sure of himself. I'm touching him. He's just standing there, looking at me. His eyes are little and friendly. His fur is not as coarse as I thought it would be. It's crimped and wavy on the ends. I'm touching his paw. The pad is rough and sturdy. There's so much strength in that paw. He could knock over the street light if he wanted to. There's such male energy about him.)

Lil: Would you prefer to drive?
Bear: I'd rather you drive so I can sit and watch things go by.

(Now we're in the car and I'm looking at him through the rearview mirror.)

Lil: Where do we go from here?
Bear: You're the one driving. You're really in control, you know.
Lil: Do you have a name?
Bear: No, no name.
Lil: Have we met before?
Bear: Lots of times. I've taken on different personalities. I haven't always been this nice.

(Oh, I just thought of my father and how angry he could be. And now I remember I gave my father a little ceramic bear with his hands on his hips when I was eight years old. He kept it on his desk with my note that said, "Dad, this reminds me of you when you are mad at me." I wonder if he still has it. I'd love to see it.)

Bear: I could be your papa bear.
Lil: Is there anything else you want to say to me?
Bear: Slow down. Take it easy on the curves.
Lil: Why do you wear a red bandanna around your neck?
Bear: It keeps me connected.
Lil: I hope you'll come back again.
Bear: It's cool. Everything's cool.

To end the active imagination session, Lil took a few deep breaths and brought her awareness completely back to the room around her. She said she'd always wanted to touch a bear, and it had felt wonderful to be able to do so. The bear's physical sturdiness modeled the inner strength she wanted for herself.

She hadn't expected her father to pop into her mind as he did. He had been a different kind of papa bear. She commented that she hadn't thought about that ceramic bear in years. And it touched her to remember what a cool kid she'd been to choose that way to comment on her father's anger.

Lil emerged from the exercise feeling warmed and connected. That very simple encounter had validated her, given her a strong ally in the bear and raised important issues for her to explore, just as she had once explored the Castro. And the bear goes with her.

This brief active imagination is a good example of how dream work can go. Dreams are touching and obscure at the same time. Often, surprising associations will occur. Dream images answer questions when they choose to and don't when they prefer not to. The imaginal figures will not be forced to say anything they don't organically mean to say.

The dreamer is emotionally and physically engaged in the scene at the same time that she is tracking the conversation with her intellect.

Active imagination is a powerful tool for tapping the unconscious through dreams. When dealing with very sensitive or overwhelming issues, it's a good idea to use this technique with support from a friend or from a therapist.

Let's return to my Day at the Beach dream. And this time, I'll imagine myself having a conversation with the caveman. I sit and relax for a few moments, do some breathing, some stretches to calm myself and clear my mind. Then I return to the dream scene and sit down opposite the man.

I find, as I settle in, that the game, the parallel lines, are still hooking my interest much more than any other element in the scene, including the man. So I decide to talk with the game. Remember, our restrictions about what is animate or inanimate don't exist in the imaginal. Here is the dialogue as it unfolded.

> *Emma:* You intrigue me. I like that you don't try to explain yourself, that you exist just as you are with no apology. Like a mystery that is allowed to continue to be a mystery. Like a piece of art that doesn't exhaust itself. It just is. Tell me about yourself.
>
> *Game:* I am very simple things. Lines and space and roundness. Simplicity and mystery, motion and stillness. Union of opposites. I'm the elemental experience under all the living. I take you back to basics where answers don't exist the way they do in the thinking world. And that generates a sense of belonging, doesn't it?
>
> *Emma:* Yeah. I feel drawn in. I feel a sense of awe at just being able to experience life. But I'm writing a book and I need something a little more definite.
>
> *Game:* That is so funny. I am not an amusement park or an encyclopedia. Go in the opposite direction. Try less. Be present more. That could be enough, you know! I've already given you a

lot to think about.

Emma: OK. Is this dream about how to handle dreams?

Game: Yes, about that and about many other things. It's about underlying processes. Constant interactions. Stillness and motion.

Emma: That gives me something to think about.

I come away with the sense that I've seen beneath the surface of things and felt the vitality of the basic urge that makes everything go. But as you can see in the dialogue, I really wanted a taut, left-brained statement to bring back. In spite of knowing better, I wanted my idea of "The Answer." "The Right Answer." When that wish is not satisfied in this interaction, I find I can settle into the scene and be touched by its simple beauty. I take these thoughts and feelings into my day.

In the hours after the exercise, I found myself wondering where there is awe in my daily life. The truth is that I don't leave much time for awe. I'm busy doing a good job and hurrying to the next thing. I figure things out, I don't stand in front of them and wonder at their mystery. Oops. There it is. A kind of . . . meaning. An answer. This dream is about standing in front of things and appreciating their mystery.

What would happen if I at least paused to be with the mystery of things before I plunge into solving them or finishing them or doing whatever I do to them? What awes me? How can I make more room for it in my life?

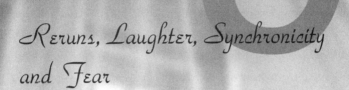

Reruns, Laughter, Synchronicity and Fear

"A man is shown in his dreams what he thinks in his heart."

—Rabbi Jonathan

Feelings, Good and Bad

I once worked with a young woman in her 20s who had a very active dream life. She said it had always been that way for her. But of all her dream experiences, she most treasured those occasional mornings when she actually laughed herself awake. She described the experience.

As I begin to awaken, I become conscious of a sound, and then I realize it is me and I am laughing. I realize my shoulders are shaking, and then I become aware of the most amazing feeling of lightness and pure gladness. It's not the usual good feeling we have when we're laughing. It has something different about it. It's a happiness way down in the belly, a whole body amusement with surprise woven into it. Most of the time I don't remember what I'm laughing at but that doesn't matter. In fact, it makes it even better! Being drawn into consciousness that way . . . it's like a painless birth. The joy of it has an innocence and a gladness I've never felt at any other time.

As we dream, the busiest part of the brain is the emotional center, the amygdaloid complex, which is associated with processing emotions and emotional memory. The feelings unleashed by dreams can increase blood pressure and heart rate, cause perspiration and sexual arousal, and even awaken the dreamer.

Here's a dream that involves several different emotions from a 50-year-old woman named Eileen. The dream tells the story of the end of one way of life and the beginning of another:

There is a dream which I delight in and long for when I'm writing. It means to me that the work is going well. . . . I dream of a very tall building. It's in the process of being built and there are scaffolds and steps. . . . I'm climbing it with alacrity and joy and laughter. . . . I can't tell you how delicious that is.

～ ～ Maya Angelou

In my dream, I am awakening because I have to go to the bathroom. As I begin to sit up, I noticed the covers are mounded over my huge belly. I know I can't be pregnant, but I am very confused; I'm normally thin. What happened? As I flip the covers off, I am surprised to find my arm is a flipper. It dawns on me: "Uh-oh, I've become a manatee." I flump out of bed with a huge thud and waddle into the hallway, my eyes accustoming themselves to the darkness.

As I stand at the bathroom doorway, I wonder how I'd actually get up on the john. Then the thought occurs to me, "Hey, wait a minute. If I'm a manatee, I really don't need to bother using the toilet." I look longingly at my toothbrush though; my teeth feel pretty fuzzy. I understand it is futile; I'll never be able to brush my teeth. The life I've known is over. I couldn't, of course, stay married. We have two teenage daughters, and it would be scandalous if their father was married to an animal.

I suddenly become alarmed: Manatees are water creatures. I'm not even sure they can breathe air. Then I relax because I realize I am a dream manatee, and in my dreams, I can do anything.

I need to leave home. I look down the darkened stairway, pull my flippers in and go scooting down head first, thumping all the way. I'm so blubbery, it doesn't hurt a bit. I wander around, saying good-bye to the life I've known.

The front door opens wide and I go outside. Dawn is breaking, and everything has that rosy glow. By the curb, I see eight or nine large brown leaf-recycling bags nestled side-by-side. I remember that walruses sleep all piled together. I decide to go out and sleep there. I find a comfy place with the large bags cuddled around me. Then I have this thought, "Look at this, wherever you go, the universe makes a home for you." Then I drift off to sleep.

At this point, I awaken, laughing out loud.

Eileen reported an array of feelings: surprise, bewilderment, sadness, regret, excitement and finally, contentment. When she retold the dream, she glowed with pleasure at the adventure and the excitement of having a new body, and such an unusual one. Her gladness mimicked the fullness of the manatee itself, and her dream illustrates the fluid nature of emotion. Always moving, always changing.

In ancient Mesopotamia, a dreamer could tell his dream to a reed and then burn it, destroying both the reed and the emotional power of the dream.

Van de Castle

Joyful dreams like Eileen's are actually reported much less often than darker dreams. In *Getting a Grip on Dreams*, Ennis and Parker cite research showing that only about 20 percent of dream emotions are happy. That may be because dreams containing fear and anxiety stir self-preservation instincts, and those dreams are likely to be more pressing and so more frequently remembered.

Several research studies on nightmare sufferers reported that they tended to have creative jobs or lifestyles and described themselves as empathic and emotionally sensitive. The nightmare subjects recalled stormy adolescences and described an adult style of openness and acceptance. They were not especially anxious people but could be described as having thinner boundaries than others do between themselves and the outer world.

In our waking lives, emotions can be a challenge. We've learned to divide feelings into good and bad. We try to drop anchor in the positives, while we call the negatives moral failures. If, as Jung thought, dreams are sometimes compensation for elements missing in waking consciousness, it's no wonder our dreams are fraught with anxiety, anger and fear.

Charles, a 24-year-old graduate student, talked about this dream.

I'm at a meeting, and as I leave, I run into my brother. He's older than I am and has always teased me and put down everything I've accomplished. For some reason, at this encounter I stand right in front of him and tell him how angry I am at the way he treats me. My voice is firm. I stay in possession of myself and don't get drawn into rage with him. I say, "I think you are a mean person." He says nothing. And I walk away feeling calm and satisfied.

Charles woke from the dream feeling calm, collected and proud—even smug—at the way he'd handled his brother. He wanted to examine that, so I suggested he step back into the dream as observer. He imagined himself standing with them, noticing their positions via each other. "They're squared off," he said. "I stood directly in front of my brother, eye to eye, shoulder to shoulder."

I suggested he say more about that physical positioning. Once again I simply followed his interest. Charles went on to say he didn't conflict with a lot of people and hadn't known how powerful that position was. Then he laughed and shared the memory of being in dancing class as a kid and being told to mirror his partner so that they moved in sync: shoulders, trunks, and so on.

The generic message of any nightmare is: Wake up. Pay attention. There is a survival issue being brought to your attention here! Sometimes the "survival issues" raised by nightmares are related to actual physical health. Most often, however, the nightmare is trying to draw attention to questions of emotional and spiritual authenticity in the dreamer's life.

— Jeremy Taylor

When that memory came to him, Charles's attention moved from conflict to dancing. He thought about it. "My brother and I have been doing a dance—the same dance—since I can remember. When

I say it that way, it sounds like such a game. A waste of time. The same routine over and over. We're both in it. I keep the dance going, too. I guess I've always thought he ran the show. But this dream shows us as mirror images. I've never thought about it this way before. I'm not sure I like it either. I thought I had to win out over my brother and here's this new angle—that I'm responsible for myself and I have a part in the routine."

Charles had stepped into the dream, observed the action, noticed one aspect of it and accepted the association that came to him. Memory of the dance classes sparked a bit of humor, and that's where the focus shifted. He followed the dancing association and let it suggest something new to him. He discovered his part in the dance and, in subsequent conversations, explored that and possibilities for change.

In terms of emotions, the anger that had dominated the dream was dispelled in the dream work. Even the measured anger he showed needed to be gone so he could see himself apart from his brother and from their dance.

Charles would have preferred to simply be congratulated for his handling of his brother, but his psyche took him further, beyond his brother. Dream work usually goes in unexpected directions and always brings new information. The ego, manager of our daytime consciousness, usually balks at information that didn't come through rational channels, and the new idea may feel foreign at first. Then the task is to observe our behaviors in light of the new information, think and talk about it, and watch for opportunities to live it.

Emotions in dreams have dynamism unchecked by our usual self-restraints and logic. In the case of nightmares, Anthony Stevens explains that the dreamer is reacting along ancient response patterns of fight, flight or freeze in the face of fearful stimuli in the environment. He goes on to say that earlier in our evolution, major sources

of threat were predatory animals and hostile strangers, and these figures still predominate in contemporary nightmares—as do poten-
tially dangerous situations, such
as being exposed without cover
in open spaces, being trapped in
a confined area with no means
of escape, being alone in the
dark, or being high up and in
danger of falling. He adds that
nightmares can serve the pur-
pose of sharpening our survival instincts. Working with nightmares
gives us an opportunity to learn new ways of coping that we can
transfer to our waking life.

> *The image . . . is the teacher, and*
> *you have to control your*
> *interpretative zeal if you are to*
> *"hear" the image and discover*
> *the part of yourself inside it.*
>
> James Hillman

Let's look at a nightmare reported by a young woman named Liz:

> *I walked into a room, an auditorium. My colleague and friend came*
> *with me. We each carried a hammer, the kind that's used in upholstery.*
> *I set my pocketbook on a long table. Two men came into the room. They*
> *each had hammers, too. They walked toward the table, and I got worried*
> *that one of them would steal the money out of my purse, which was lying*
> *there open. He began poking at my bag with his hammer. I did it back*
> *to him. My colleague and his friend just stood there and watched.*
> *Suddenly, the lights went out. I got so frightened, I screamed. That's*
> *when I woke up.*

There was another interesting detail. Liz's husband reported that
he had heard her whimpering and had turned over and laid his arm
around her waist just before she began to scream. So the dreamer's
experience with the images was supplemented and probably intensi-
fied by the physical contact she received from her husband.

Liz had consulted her dream dictionary and learned that the
intensity of the fear she'd felt indicated the importance of the

message the dream was bringing. We talked about that idea and about the dream, but without much excitement. Even the feeling of threat that had accompanied the dream had vanished. I asked her to

Our unconscious existence is the real one and our conscious world a kind of illusion.

C. G. Jung

describe the scene again. She drew a diagram that showed where everyone was standing. She described the others. Her colleague and his friend didn't do anything. "They just stood

there like witnesses," she said. "The other man . . . why did he keep poking at my purse? Why is he carrying a hammer?" Liz said she didn't have any associations to hammers.

As we talked, she returned to the purse, the money and that man. So I followed her interest. "What does money mean to you?" I asked. "Freedom," she responded instantaneously. It was the first real energy I'd heard. Her association of money with freedom was moving our understanding ahead. We wandered around a bit more. She commented that she didn't feel physically threatened by the man. He made no effort to come after her. He simply poked at the purse. We puzzled over that behavior. I explained that one way to approach dream images is to assume that each is a part of the dreamer, some aspect of the dreamer's personality.

That surprised Liz. Like most everyone else, she identified with her dream self in her dreams. She stopped to consider. When a character in a dream has been identified as the bad one, it is difficult to see it as part of oneself. I explained that part of the work with this dream would be to open communication between her dream self and the would-be thief. "Oh," she responded, again with increased excitement. "He wants freedom, too!" Amazement at what had popped out of her mouth danced across Liz's face. And she began to think about the would-be thief aspect of herself who did not have the freedom he craved. She had moved beyond the good/bad dichotomy and was beginning to understand this image.

We knew we were on the right track because of the emotion that arose. Liz felt spontaneous interest and excitement grip her. Something clicked. She didn't figure out the dream. She experienced it, began to understand the thief and became conscious of this dimension of the situation. And that immediate experience led to a shift in her understanding of herself. She, too, wanted freedom of some kind.

Psychologist Eugene Gendlin would call her spontaneous insight a "felt sense." A felt sense is a combined cognitive, physical and emotional response. Thoughts, a bodily sense of rightness and an emotional satisfaction unite at the unveiling of a truth. Felt sense is not created by thinking the issue through or by gathering facts. It springs full-blown from the experience. Liz entered into the reality of the thief and that engagement bloomed into an "aha."

Gendlin's work with the concept of felt sense is central to working with dreams. To understand what I mean by felt sense, imagine for a minute that you are standing before two doors. The first door opens and there you see your dearest friend. Notice how you feel. What is the emotion? What are the body sensations that go with that emotion? Do any thoughts come to mind? When I imagine seeing my friend, I'm happy. That translates to a slowing of my breathing, a feeling of warmth in my chest, a letting go in my muscles. I relax. I think, "Oh, good. It's Sasha." That whole experience is a felt sense.

Dreams are not disguised wishfulfillments but show the situation exactly as it is.

    Edward C. Whitmont

Now, imagine the second door opens and you see someone with whom you have some unfinished business. What's your emotion?

And how does your body feel? What do you think? When I imagine my person, I feel a bit anxious, a bit cautious. My throat tightens some, the muscles in my face tighten, too. I feel "on alert." I'm wondering what the person will say. All of that, too, is a felt sense.

The felt sense keeps us honest. While we can override our emotions or our thoughts, it isn't possible to deny our physical responses. A tingling, a twitch, muscle relaxation, butterflies in the stomach, a sudden sleepiness, a sigh—all can be part of a felt sense trying to make itself clear. The body doesn't lie and can be our greatest ally in understanding ourselves and our dreams.

Liz's felt sense came in excitement, relief and words. It confirmed that she had found an important part of herself in meeting the thief and grasping his motivation. The mind-body is giving us felt senses all the time in response to external and imaginal people and events. The stirring of a felt sense indicates that this image has juice and needs attention. At those moments your mind-body is the best and only dream dictionary you need.

In Liz's case, the significant fright in the dream came when the lights went out, but the first round of dream work took us in another direction. If she chose to, she could return to that aspect of the dream at another time. It's not unusual to visit and revisit dreams to mine them for more and more of their riches.

Reruns

Van de Castle, in *Our Dreaming Mind*, reports that two-thirds of adults experience recurrent dreams. These series can stretch over years and lifetimes: being chased, traveling home, attending a family event, taking an exam, trying to make a phone call. These dreams usually have an element of stress to them. Jung believed that recurrent dreams picture a central conflict as yet unsolved, and dream expert Jeremy Taylor agrees that "Recurrent dreams tend to be about the deeper layers of the dreamer's personal 'myth'—that essential, archetypal, symbolic story that a person tends to act out, over and over again in various forms, over the course of his or her entire life." Rosalind Cartwright has found that the ending of a dream series may indicate some mastery of the issue has been attained.

[Owning all aspects of the dream] is a way to become more familiar with how it feels to know something by identifying with it rather than describing or talking about it.

Frances E. Vaughan

Joanie, a newly divorced woman in her late 30s, reported a series of 10 dreams that extended back five or six years.

All the dreams are about a big, very old decaying house. It belongs to an acquaintance of the family, and it isn't kept up. Each dream begins differently, but I always end up in the attic. It isn't like a real attic would be. There are lots of levels, lots of small rooms, tunnels, secret passageways, thick curtains. Like a maze. It has a claustrophobic feel and there are lots of dark, dirty, dusty spaces and a lot of stuff.

Each time I remember that I've been there before. I always go with one or two others who leave me there. I feel alarmed and hesitant, but curious. I want to explore, but I don't have a flashlight and could get hurt. I know there is something extremely dangerous in there someplace. I tiptoe into areas, then someone calls me away.

In the most recent dream, I meet my father and sister in the garden, with intention of going in to see the house. This is the first time I remember being downstairs. All the rooms are emptied out. Some walls are down so you can see bare joists and woodwork. Some floors are unsafe because rotten wood has been removed. There's a purpose to our being there but it's not quite clear. I might have been thinking of buying it. Going through, I become aware of other people, owners, whom we did sort of know. They're behind us, keeping tabs on us. I don't have a good feeling about them, but I don't feel threatened. These are people to be avoided.

We find the attic all cleared out. It's not familiar initially. Then I think, "Oh, this is the attic I've been in many times." All the stuff is gone. You can see where walls have been taken down. It's dirty and dusty but not claustrophobic anymore. Now it's a BIG open space with sunlight coming through the windows.

My father is making comments about the construction and the work that's been done. He's indicating this was a massive project.

I'm so surprised that this is that place I'd been in that was so ominous. Now it's just this big, empty space and doesn't seem treacherous. All the danger has been removed. Someone has done a lot of work here.

When we talked, it had been a year since Joanie had this dream, and we thought she had probably come to the end of the series. She could still feel her amazement at finding the attic cleared out and bright. She was most struck by how compelled she'd felt to come to this attic again and again to explore, even in the presence of danger. I asked about the period of her life during which she'd been having these dreams and she described a very difficult time. During it, she'd realized that she had to end her marriage. She'd been in psychotherapy herself, exploring her history and developing skills to cope with the separation and divorce. She'd resumed her education and begun a business. She'd survived the dating scene and gotten clearer on what was important for her in a relationship.

The dream seemed to summarize the changes in Joanie and in her life. Her conscious hard work had created openness and light in herself where there'd once been darkness and dust. And the dream pictured the present as a lighted, open space as yet uninhabited. The last dream also enlarges her consciousness to include the whole house and its potential.

More clearly than the individual dream, a series displays the elegant weave that every problem is: strands of meaning, emotion, experience and belief.

Here are three dreams from another series:

A variety of dream elements may repeat: a theme, a symbol, a character, an emotion or even a vague sensing. In whatever form, repetitive dreams clearly get our attention.

Kathleen Sullivan

1. I am in the monastery again. A bad snowstorm is coming, and I am worried about whether I should leave. One of my friends had gotten to go out, and he picked up the mail. There was a package for me. It was a spring bulb for me to plant. It was already in the planting mixture.

2. I have returned to the monastery. We have just become novices, and it is the first day of doing the chores and wearing the habit. But all of this is happening at the house where I grew up. I am unsure of where things are. I see a woman I want to spend time with, but I don't know if she would be interested. She seems withdrawn. Then I am leading her through a very crowded subway, trying to get back to the monastery/home in time for breakfast duties.

3. I've entered the monastery again and am feeling very unhappy and angry and penned up. I am with a huge gathering of monks. We young ones are proceeding to the chapel. Some of us have taken our sandals off to be more comfortable and we still have them off. I want to be in line behind one of my friends. It also seems that women are there but I cannot see them.

These dreams came from David, a 28-year-old man who had spent a few years in a Trappist monastery early in his adulthood.

Though he had left the monastery more than five years earlier, he continued to have dreams of returning there. The dreams irritated him; he could not understand why they continued. He had established his life in the world, and except for the depression that had brought him in to treatment, he was reasonably happy and had no regrets, either about going to the monastery or about leaving it. He maintained a vital spiritual life but didn't participate in organized religion.

In his dream series, he had entered and left and reentered and was thinking about leaving again and wondering if he would then want to return. Confusion and indecision were a common thread. Often, he was wandering the halls, trying to figure out what to do or talking with his advisor or getting lost on the grounds. Over a period of five years, two of which he spent in therapy, he had about eleven monastery dreams.

David associated the monastery to longing, striving, contentment, judgment, shame, self-denial, indecision and emotional dullness. His comings and goings reminded him of conflicts between earthliness and spirituality, individual and community, self-sacrifice and self-expression. In working with the monastery series, David tended to a wide web of central issues in his life.

He had no one "aha" moment when the dreams stopped, but they did stop. David came in for a few sessions to examine the series when he had been about a year without one. As we looked over the dreams, he commented that the squirrelly, questioning

Yet this other life has its interests, its gaieties, its satisfactions. . . . Daft or wise, terrible or exquisite, it is a further helping of experience, a bonus after dark, another slice of life cut differently, for which, it seems to me, we are never sufficiently grateful. Only a dream? Why only?

J. B. Priestley

feeling that repeated across the series reminded him of a kind of
anxiety he felt when he drove himself unrealistically or criticized
himself for not having an answer for a problem. The entrapment created by that attitude was as real as the locked gate of a monastery.
And the sense of shame when he didn't get something right led back
to experiences in his early, strict Catholic education. Overall, the
dreams wove together his hunger for a genuine way of life with the
obsessive, looping and impotent behaviors that blocked his way.
David got a look at how he was drawn to overwork and overworry
about reaching some idea of perfection. Into the monastery and out
again. Over and over.

Because David highly valued the spiritual quest, his psyche used
it to underscore that any shame-driven effort in his life was futile.

David felt he had become more present to himself, more compas-
sionate with all he found there. His self-image shifted from being
that of a hard worker to that of a confident man. He still longed and
strove, but a satisfaction had grown stronger in him, and that
changed the quality of the striving.

Should David return in five years with the same series, he will be
able to find other lessons in its images. Dreams, you'll remember, are
like multifaceted gems. Depending on the light and where you look,
the view will be different. It can be disorienting to have one interpretation turn another on its head. But the nature of dreams and of that
part of us where they come from is infinitely in process. Opposites
reconcile, everything moves toward wholeness.

A particular kind of recurring dream comes with a condition
called Post-Traumatic Stress Disorder. After an experience of
extreme stress, the psyche struggles to integrate the disturbing
thoughts, feelings and images connected with the event. One way it
does this is through dreams.

In *The Wisdom of the Dream*, Merrill Berger and Stephen Segaller

84   Waking Your Dreams

The transformation of frightening dream images is similar to what commonly occurs in fairy tales: the frog becomes a prince, the beast a handsome young man. . . .

         ~ ~ James A. Hall, MD

report on the work of Dr. Harry Wilmer of Salado, Texas. Wilmer is an analyst, trained in both Freudian and Jungian theories. From the Vietnam veterans he works with, he has collected 350 dreams of that war. They are difficult dreams, character-ized by horror, killing and mutilation.

In working with repetitive nightmares, Wilmer reports that at first the dreams are realistic, recounting events that either happened or could have happened in the war. Then as the therapy work progresses, the veteran can have what Wilmer calls a "healing nightmare" in which a new element is introduced into the dream. He tells of one dream that changed to include his (Wilmer's) presence on the battlefield with the veteran whom he was helping. The introduction of that new element indicated that the psyche was kicking in, that the archetypal horror was being processed and digested. With that new element, the dream became workable and not simply a frozen repetition of terror.

Synchronicity

A synchronicity is a meaningful coincidence. An event in the psyche seems to burst out of the imaginal world and appear in the normal flow of rational existence. An inner event connects with an outer event. One does not cause the other, but they are related in that they share a meaning. A synchronicity confirms that what is going on inside us is one with what is happening outside us. The veil between the imaginal world and the world of matter lifts and unity is clear. Synchronicities are not magic. They are the normal elbowing of one realm up against the other, moments of feeling at home in a much larger context than we usually perceive. They usually occur when an individual is experiencing a significant developmental phase or a period of intense emotion.

The unconscious image can come as an idea, a premonition or a dream. Here is an example of a synchronicity that occurred in relation to a dream.

A middle-aged woman went to Assisi, Italy, to attend a workshop on fiction writing. After getting settled in her hotel, she napped and had this dream.

With two other women, I am singing "Over the Rainbow" and flying in circles around the room, not far off the ground. At first I worry that now I would discover I really can't sing on key. But I get over it and get into the singing.

Rose chuckled that she worried about singing off-key when something as remarkable as flying was occurring.

Later that evening, she joined about 25 other American writers and artists for cocktails. She recalls that she met two women who shared her distaste for getting-to-know-you events, so they slipped out for the best pizza any of them ever expected to eat.

. . . the occurrence of synchronistic dreams are evidence of a close connection between the unconscious of one person and that of another. They may also be taken as evidence that the unconscious is less limited in time and space than the conscious mind.

— James A. Hall, MD

Next morning, Rose went into the town in search of writing paper. She climbed the long hill to the Piazza del Commune, passed the outdoor cafés and the central fountain and ran into Katherine, one of the women from the night before. She, too, was in search of the stationery store, so they asked directions and finally found the shop well beyond the tourist section, out on the edge of town where real life went on.

It was a good stationery store: beautiful Italian paper, fine inks and journals. A paper junkie's heaven! As Rose wandered the aisles, something very strange happened. The background music changed and "Over the Rainbow" filled the store. She shook her head to make sure she was hearing correctly. What were the odds? She found Katherine, blathered out the dream and told her to listen to the music. Then they went in search of their third friend—Joanne from the last night's supper—to share their adventure.

Rose had been touched by her synchronistic experience. It brought strong feelings: contentment, confidence, a strong sense of belonging, not just to the new circle of friends but to a forward-moving energy. She felt whole, more dedicated to her writing and sure of her success at it. Taking the trip had been a gesture of confidence in the future, and the synchronicity underlined its importance.

That time in Italy marked the beginning of a circle of important friendships, and it also marked the beginning of Rose's identity as a writer.

I've heard descriptions of many synchronicities. A man dreamed of a woman he'd never seen before and sat next to her on a transatlantic flight the next day. A woman dreamed of a lion, and the next morning her daughter reached into the depths of her toy box and gave her the gift of a small rubber lion. He is fierce and faithful and stands guard in her study. A woman dreamed of a table spread with food and later that week was unexpectedly invited to a picnic, where she again saw the table. A synchronicity is a powerful reminder that the imaginal world and what we call the real world are separate only in our conception of them.

READER/CUSTOMER CARE SURVEY

We care about your opinions! Please take a moment to fill out our online Reader Survey at **http://survey.hcibooks.com.**

As a **"THANK YOU"** you will receive a **VALUABLE INSTANT COUPON** towards future book purchases as well as a **SPECIAL GIFT** available only online! Or, you may mail this card back to us and we will send you a copy of our exciting catalog with your valuable coupon inside.

(PLEASE PRINT IN ALL CAPS)

First Name _____ MI. _____ Last Name _____

Address _____

State _____ Zip _____ Email _____ City _____

1. Gender
☐ Female ☐ Male

2. Age
☐ 8 or younger
☐ 9-12 ☐ 13-16
☐ 17-20 ☐ 21-30
☐ 31+

3. Did you receive this book as a gift?
☐ Yes ☐ No

4. Annual Household Income
☐ under $25,000
☐ $25,000 - $34,999
☐ $35,000 - $49,999
☐ $50,000 - $74,999
☐ over $75,000

5. What are the ages of the children living in your house?
☐ 0 - 14 ☐ 15+

6. Marital Status
☐ Single
☐ Married
☐ Divorced
☐ Widowed

7. How did you find out about the book?
(please choose one)
☐ Recommendation
☐ Store Display
☐ Online
☐ Catalog/Mailing
☐ Interview/Review

8. Where do you usually buy books?
(please choose one)
☐ Bookstore
☐ Online
☐ Book Club/Mail Order
☐ Price Club (Sam's Club, Costco's, etc.)
☐ Retail Store (Target, Wal-Mart, etc.)

9. What subject do you enjoy reading about the most?
(please choose one)
☐ Parenting/Family
☐ Relationships
☐ Recovery/Addictions
☐ Health/Nutrition
☐ Christianity
☐ Spirituality/Inspiration
☐ Business Self-help
☐ Women's Issues
☐ Sports

10. What attracts you most to a book?
(please choose one)
☐ Title
☐ Cover Design
☐ Author
☐ Content

HEFG

TAPE IN MIDDLE; DO NOT STAPLE

BUSINESS REPLY MAIL
FIRST-CLASS MAIL PERMIT NO 45 DEERFIELD BEACH, FL

POSTAGE WILL BE PAID BY ADDRESSEE

Health Communications, Inc.
3201 SW 15th Street
Deerfield Beach FL 33442-9875

FOLD HERE

Comments

Daydreams

"As a child you are given dream time as part of your fictional life. Into your hands go the books of dream travel, Dorothy's dream travel, the Darling family's dream travel in Peter Pan, the children of Narnia. . . .

"And then at the age of five or something like that, they start to teach you the gross national product of Chile. And you're left thinking, Wait! What happened to Oz and Never-Never Land and Narnia? Are they no longer relevant? One of the things you're taught is No! they are no longer relevant. . . .

"You're going to be taught to compete, very often for spurious reasons. You are going to be taught that the accrual of facts, however unimportant those facts are, will somehow make you better and more able to deal with the world. You're going to be told that the only way the world works is through the waking life. . . .

"All those things are lies."

—Clive Barker

From "Airy Nothing"

As a kid, I held a very specific view of the universe. God owned the sky, Eisenhower owned the country, my father owned the Arco Chemical Company where he worked and Walt Disney owned imagination.

While the others were busy managing their quadrants of reality, Disney wove stories for children: Cinderella and her stepsisters, *Peter Pan*, the ugly duckling, Snow White and terrifying witches. I understood—well, except for the witches—that it was all make-believe. Pretend was like the icing on birthday cakes, essential but ephemeral. In the real world, what counted was being good and being smart. The imaginary world of witches and pixie dust was the anteroom where we children played while waiting to grow up.

Daydreaming begins early in life, takes many forms and serves many purposes along the way. Very young children use imaginative play to integrate the external world, its characters, customs and events into memory. They play at the life they observe going on around them and daydream themselves into it. Children also create worlds in which they can shape reality. I imagined a world without elementary school, piano lessons or girl cliques. There were no Monday mornings, day camps or dentist appointments. I could curl around a new book every day, enjoy a steady supply of chocolate-covered pretzels, spend the whole summer at the beach and be the prettiest girl in the neighborhood. I daydreamed about being a doctor, a nurse, a teacher, an actress, a trapeze artist and a writer. I imagined which aunt I would go to live with if anything ever happened to my parents. I imagined being able to walk on the ceiling. I conjured my own passionately devoted Prince Charmings, and I pictured huge birthday parties with loving friends. In the absolute privacy and authority of those daydreams, I was not waiting around for anything. I was practicing my own life.

Daydreaming peaks in adolescence as teens assemble possibilities for the future. Daydreams are practice, they are trial runs, opportunities to expand, experiment and play at no risk. In his classic *Daydreaming,* Jerome Singer reports research showing that adult interests and occupations often grow out of those adolescent fantasies.

He also reports that oldest and only children seem to daydream more than others and that children with the capacity to incorporate fantasy into play seem to enjoy themselves more and are able to concentrate better.

If my thought-dreams could be seen,
They'd probably put my
head in a guillotine
But it's alright, Ma, it's
life and life only.

Bob Dylan

Daydreams in adulthood range over a myriad of topics, which Singer identifies as largely to do with practical real-life matters but also include sexual pleasure, good luck, magical good fortune and heroism. On a dreary winter afternoon, a highly unscientific survey of friends turned up these subjects of daydreams: a new house, a new office, long uninterrupted naps, nude sunbathing, a bowl of chocolate frosting, the wide-open skies of Idaho, loved ones, tropical islands, accomplishments, love.

Daydreaming appears as any of a variety of nonlinear types of thought, none of which are exactly connected with the here and now. Privacy is daydreaming's most striking characteristic. We can do it without anyone's knowing, anywhere and at anytime. It's like carrying a miniature television with infinite programming within ourselves—except better. Daydreaming lives on the frontiers of our waking consciousness, pushing it endlessly outward. We are so used to our daydream's presence in our consciousness, we forget to appreciate the dazzling tool that it is. Daydreams can achieve what seems impossible and create material reality from "airy nothing." Yesterday you imagined a hiking vacation in the red-rock country of Arizona, and tomorrow you go online and make reservations with a tour group that will enable you to do exactly that. What began in your daydream ends as solid reality under your feet.

Daydreams share the language and power of imagery with night dreams, and it is in pictures that most daydreams occur. But we also daydream about abstractions as in philosophy or religion, world peace or environmental preservation.

Daydreaming comes as reverie and reminiscence, as "what if" and pretend, as worry and grief. It blossoms in the arts, business innovation, prayer and plans for the future. It can remove us entirely from the present and show replays of a magical vacation or a frustrating argument. It can propel us into the future or into some fantastic parallel universe.

> *It is important to have a secret, a premonition of things unknown. It fills life with something impersonal, a numinosum. A man who has never experienced that has missed something important. . . . Not everything which happens can be anticipated. The unexpected and the incredible belong in this world.*
>
> ⚮ ⚮ C. G. Jung

Daydreaming takes many forms. Most subtle is that stream of consciousness, the inner conversation and commentary, that accompanies us through our days. It is so ubiquitous that it is sometimes hard to identify.

If you've ever done any kind of meditation, you are aware of it. Or if you watch your mind's activity during a straightforward task, like driving a car or putting away groceries or waiting for a train, you will hear this stream of consciousness wending its way through the background.

Right now, if you put this book down, choose an object in the room and focus your awareness on it for one minute, you will see, in the form of distractions, this parade of unsolicited thought. When I tried it, I looked over at a purple vase I received last Christmas as a gift. For one minute I gazed at the vase. Here's what I noticed going through my mind: "Brenda's gift . . . Should I keep it in this room? . . . Should I put it away for a while? . . . Am I doing this right?. . . I love that color . . . The design looks like a wave . . . It's shiny . . . This light is so flat . . . I'm tired of winter . . . No sign of crocuses yet . . . I'll need to do some landscaping on the side of the house this year . . . How smooth the vase looks . . . Am I doing this right? . . . What will I bring to the party later? . . . Why was I feeling so tired this morning? . . . Here I am looking at this vase . . . Is the minute up yet?"

Your litany may be similar or more far-ranging. These streams of thought can associate far away from the starting point. An exercise like this belies our belief that we are single-minded beings and underscores what psychologist Jerome Singer calls "layers of thought" active in our waking minds. We can straddle several realities at once. I can be here at my desk, writing, looking into the woods and listening to one lone, chirping robin and at the same time, remember standing on the beach of an Italian island, fingering a brown sponge I'd just scooped from the warm water. I can make a pot of tea as I imagine myself in the grit and bustle of London's Piccadilly Circus or bicycling along the flat, quiet roads of Nantucket's interior. Our capacity to imagine in this way is dazzling. It can greatly enrich life once we've learned to recognize it. Observing stream of consciousness daydreams reveals preoccupations, interests, fears and worries that we may not be completely aware of, and in that way, deepens our understanding of ourselves.

That's the heart of why daydreaming is so important: It tells the other half of the story. We act in the world, and as we do, the imaginal stream feeds or acts at cross-purposes to our lives' activity. If we know our daydreams, we are awake. If we can integrate them, we are vastly enriched. A session I had with a client named Saul illustrates my point.

As he settled down on the sofa, Saul commented that he was feeling scattered. In fact, he said he had completely missed a turn on the way to the office because he was off daydreaming. I asked where, and he described himself ensconced with a mug of delicious coffee in the observation car of a train as it crossed through the Rocky Mountains. He was dazzled by the views and the broad blue sky. As he spoke, the spell the daydream had cast remained fresh. Rather than being scattered, he seemed firmly rooted in his fantasy.

Pay attention to your fantasies. . . .
They are not only making sense,
but they are sense-making.

＞＜ ＞＜ Andrew Samuels

I suggested we follow the daydream and see what it held for him. Saul settled into his imagination and talked about the views, the quiet, the soothing sound of the train under him. Mostly, it was the peacefulness that struck him. He was quiet for a few minutes, then took a deep breath and opened his eyes. "It's been years since I've had a vacation," he said. "I haven't been able to get away. I've forgotten how to stop. I thought I couldn't stop. There's too much to lose now. But I'm thinking that there is a vacation in me waiting to get out. I'd like to look into this."

Saul had been struggling with the workaholism that had dominated his life for many years. Troubling physical symptoms indicated that something had to change in his routine, but he had been unable to significantly alter his behavior. Luckily, this daydream emerged to snag his attention and lure him into new possibilities.

Daydreaming undergirds the multitasking that is so much a part of our lives. I can simultaneously sit in the dentist's chair for crown work and assemble the shopping list of items I'll pick up at the market on the way home. I can monitor the stops on the train that takes me into the city while I count stitches on the scarf I'm crocheting and imagine what I'd enjoy eating for lunch.

Daydreaming involves the whole person in a way that thought does not. Rational thinking proceeds from known to unknown. It stays on track. I can almost hear the brain grinding away as I describe it. Daydreaming, or fantasizing, is more of a dialogue between linear-directed thought and the mysterious voice of imagination that delivers unexpected ideas and makes unanticipated connections. Linear thought allows the circumambulating imagination its own time and rhythms and still offers an anchorage. When linear thought and imagination work together, we have the best of both worlds.

Some daydreams develop into detailed fantasies that are helpful in managing stress, passing the time, comforting or encouraging the daydreamer. A 23-year-old client of mine who longed to live openly as a gay man was not yet ready to do that in his public life. But we discovered that every night he fell asleep to daydreams of living an openly gay life. In those fantasies, he was practicing and learning to shape the life he would someday build, and the daydreams brought him deep joy and hope. They also served to desensitize him to the judgments he knew awaited him.

Now, for me there's another kind of waking dreaming, which I call doodling. . . . On occasions, I'll sit down and make a picture not knowing what I'm making. . . . That often becomes a crystalization and a clarification of a lot of what's going on in my head. . . . A lot of random stuff sticks together, coalesces to make something that has its own logic.

       Art Spiegelman

Longstanding daydreams tend to be more positive than negative. They are also the imaginal eye on the waking world that refuses to let the density and sway of what appears to be to have the final say. Like night dreams, daydreams remind us of our fluid, indefatigable aspects that are naturally on the move, always developing toward wholeness. And like night dreams, daydreams get a bad rap for being frivolous wastes of time.

A client described this incident that had happened at work. One day she was looking out her office window, thinking about a project she wanted to launch. It was that meandering kind of thought, an idea here, an idea there. Suddenly, there was a stir behind her and she heard a sharp clap. Her boss had tiptoed into the room, come up behind her and clapped his hands to break her reverie. It was done half in fun, but that gesture captured the hostile dynamic that exists between hardworking, rational thought and the wandering receptive consideration of possibilities that is daydreaming.

Along with our private daydreaming, we also participate in cultural daydreams that create another layer of experience. In his essay "Psychiatry and the Sacred," philosopher Jacob Needleman explores the idea that our waking consciousness is a kind of socially created and approved trance. Like our stream of consciousness narratives, that trance or daydream is so familiar that we take it as a given. Shared daydreams show up in beliefs like hard work leads to success, or in movements like patriotism or party affiliation. A shared daydream of spiritual fanaticism can lead to bullying or terrorism, which then engenders another daydream of righteousness and revenge. Shared daydreams about youth and beauty engage most of us in Herculean efforts to stave off signs of aging and in denying the values associated with maturity. Daydreams on a cultural level are fine if we can remember that they are fantasies and wishes and not reality.

Practical Daydreaming

Daydreaming in a more organized form offers us a potent wellness tool. It is as if we all carry a pharmacy within us for use in times of physical and psychological stress. And the magic pill in that pharmacy is, once again, the image.

Our capacity to use the mechanics of daydreaming for healing is as ordinary as drawing breath. Somewhere along the way, we've forgotten that. Our cultural daydream imagines answers and cures coming from outside ourselves, but we can change our physical states, lower blood pressure, shift hormonal balance, enhance creativity, and reduce stress and pain through the use of daydreams. And while I can't remove my own appendix by visualizing the operation, there is plenty of data showing that I can speed my healing through the focused use of daydreaming. Leah's story illustrates what I mean.

> *Once actively accepted, a symbol can stimulate a whole palette of psychic experiences, from memories to expectations but only if we contact it emotionally. These memories can be happy or sad. The symbol frees the energy that has been blocked by the difficult memories and experiences.*
>
> Verena Kast

Leah was a 40-year-old woman who came to work through a persistent depression. During our time together, her doctor diagnosed a benign tumor on her thyroid. Leah was frightened by the prospect of major surgery and was also aware that the disruption in one of her body's creativity centers paralleled the struggles she was having in her career as a writer. As often happens, her body had mirrored an emotional issue.

Leah began preparation for the surgery with guided imagery. Guided imagery is an organized daydream. Leah's was tailored to her situation and focused on her body, particularly her throat. The imagery work included visualizing her throat, visualizing healing. The imagery work literally took her inside herself so that her throat began to be not "it" but part of her self. Imagining began to dissolve the distance between her sense of "I" and her body. She prepared tapes using the images she'd been practicing for the surgery and found a surgeon who would agree to her wish to listen to tapes during the procedure. She asked her friends to record encouragement and good wishes on the tape so that the daydream of health was strengthened by a supportive community.

After the surgery, Leah needed less than the average amount of pain medication. Her convalescence was speedy, and her surgeon expressed surprise at how quickly her scar healed.

Once she had her strength back, we explored the psychological meanings of the tumor. We talked of many things: creativity, her own individual voice, her history of being heard and not heard, her anger, doubt and alienation.

Leah had always been passionate about words. As a little girl, she'd spent hours at her old rolltop desk, writing secrets and stories. Her time at that desk never felt like work. It felt like she had come home. But years of undergraduate and graduate writing and the tedium of editing work had distanced that old love. Years of sadness and self-doubt waited to be released. She began to remember her longing to create with language and daydreamed a new dream of a life in her own words.

Eventually, Leah decided to find part-time freelance work so that she'd have freedom to develop her own voice. It sounds like a cliché, looking for freedom to develop her own voice. But she and her body had had enough of the other life. It was as if her physical self had imagined the tumor into being when no other channel for creativity was available. Leah read the metaphorical language of her body as validation of her conscious struggles, and that gave her the courage to make changes in her life.

Leah's work began to appear in literary journals, each story a sparkling, delicate gem. Now she protects her creativity and selects freelance assignments that reflect her sensibilities.

Conscious daydreams are also effective in managing pain. Arthritis, back pain, headaches, neck and jaw pain—it's all real distress. But pain perception is a sensitive measure. It reacts to beliefs, memories and to the nightmare idea that there is no way out. Pain can become a nightmarish daydream, too big to escape from. One way out is to introduce a new daydream, to change the flow of images that accompany the pain.

Paul was a 30-year-old truck driver who had injured his back and lived with persistent back pain. His doctors had advised him that he would probably have pain for the rest of his life. He couldn't work at his old job and his life was shrinking around him. He wanted to avoid surgery, so as a last resort, he came in for biofeedback. He had little hope of it working.

Biofeedback measures blood flow and warmth in the hands and at other sensitive spots on the body and feeds that information back to the client visually on a computer screen. The client can use imagery to relax. Muscles react to positive images in the mind. Blood flow and relaxation increase. And that information, delivered immediately on the screen, provides positive reinforcement for him to continue and increase the relaxation. The result is reduced pain. Paul's daydream took him to a lake where he'd fished as a child.

The desire to control the forces of nature led Paleolithic humans to create images of the world around them. If the gods made the world, then graphic imitation was a godlike act that carried with it the illusion of power.

Leonard Shlain

He imagined himself motoring out to the far side of the lake early on a summer morning. He cut the motor, and as silence fell around him, he baited his hook and dropped the line. He concentrated on the silence, on the warmth of the sun on his back, on the shimmer of the water and the fresh air. He felt the taut line connecting him to the lake's depths. He recalled the shades of green in the pines and spruces that edged the lake. His breathing slowed. The bar graphs on the screen reflected increasing relaxation, and at the end of our session, he rated his pain half the number it had been at the beginning. With practice, Paul learned to reduce his pain without the biofeedback screen. He could reenter the whole experience of the lake and was able to hold the worst of the pain at bay and reinsert himself into his life.

Paul exchanged a negative daydream for a positive one and changed his pain perception as well as the level of tension measured in his body. It sounds like magic, but it is simply the power of image used in a focused way.

As you can see, our capacity to daydream is not merely an escape hatch, but offers huge therapeutic benefits. I often spend time teaching clients to soothe and relax themselves so they can reduce daily stress and manage the stress of making changes in themselves. These visualization exercises use imaginal skills to bring the clients more deeply into their mind-bodies. Sometimes for the first time ever, they experience their muscular and nervous systems as allies in the quest to find health and wholeness.

Pearl was a 35-year-old accountant who had come in to sort through a very agitated depression. She had low-grade chronic pain from a series of sports injuries earlier in her life, so her body was not a place she automatically went to, to be soothed. I asked Pearl to recall a place where she had once felt very comfortable and contented. She smiled and said, "Cadillac Mountain in Acadia National Park." She'd vacationed once in Maine and hiked that gorgeous rocky coast. Images of the mountain and the sea were fresh in her memory. I asked her to relax and follow her breathing for a few minutes. Then I took her on an imaginal visit to Cadillac Mountain. She felt her legs climbing the stony paths, saw the fir trees, smelled the breeze, sensed the fog on her skin, listened to birds squabbling. She explored the place with all her senses, and when she was ready, she returned to full consciousness in the office.

Pearl opened her eyes with that bewildered look people often have when they emerge from an imaginal exercise like this one. By using not just memory, but the imaginal powers of her senses, Pearl changed her consciousness. She reported being more relaxed, having less physical and mental tension, and having a sense of joy that she hadn't experienced in a long time. But what most astounded her was discovering that she had the ability to imagine, to daydream herself back onto that gritty path that led to the top of the mountain.

She could feel the texture of the pine-tree bark and the intense joy of watching the fog evaporate into blue sky. Though her struggles with anxiety and depression had not evaporated, she realized she also carried untapped resources within herself that were available anytime she wanted to use them.

You can take a minute for your own daydream right now, if you'd like. Close your eyes, settle into your body, notice your breathing. Imagine a safe place you've been to or would like to visit. Now, use all your senses to experience the place. Feel the way the air touches your face. Look around. Notice the colors in the scene. Are there scents in the air? How about sounds? Nearby and in the distance? Enjoy being there. Stay as long as you'd like. Come back by opening your eyes and focusing your mind and senses again in the here and now. Notice how you feel.

Visualizing one's goals has been touted by the New Age movement as the way to manifest a new reality by seeing it first in one's imagination. Picture what you want, send it out into the universe and it will happen. "Build it and they will come." I don't think it is as simple as that. I believe that imagining creates the goal and sets the dreamer in a specific direction. But other currents in the psyche are moving in directions that may oppose the goal. There may be underground obstructions, other dreams that are saying, "No way. You can't do that. Are you crazy?" Or "That's not allowed. You're too old for that now." Major change requires coming to intuit or imagine who we really are and giving up the minor dreams that distract and obstruct.

Tara came into psychotherapy to work on anxiety that seemed to be triggered by her husband's frequent business trips. She wanted to "get rid of this anxiety, cut it out," so that she could go on with her life. Understandably, she had accumulated a lot of frustration with herself about the anxiety. She was a competent woman in her mid-20s, newly married and otherwise happy. She liked her life. Why couldn't she breeze past this?

Tara was carrying a fantasy that she could think her way out of every problem. Up until this point in her life, that had pretty much been true. But sooner or later, the benefits of linear thought run out. Tara's daydream of rational control had come to an end. I invited her to tell me about the anxiety, the actual experience of it. Could she imagine it had a shape and size and texture and weight? The question stopped her in her tracks. So many stories surrounded the anxiety by now that it was hard to touch the anxiety itself. Her thoughts circled and circled the problem.

After a few minutes, Tara cut through the thinking and touched back to the experience of the

Dear Right Brain,

Well, sweetie, I've asked you for a little help with this and I notice you're not forthcoming. I would really appreciate it if tonight you would solve this problem.

Your pal, Sue

Sue Grafton

anxiety. She said, "It's a gray-brown color. And it's like a spider's web that starts up high and seems to be dropping all around me. It has some give to it, but it is very strong. I don't think I can break it. It feels scratchy against my skin."

By creating an image of the anxiety, Tara changed an abstract idea into a sensible reality, and we began our work. Her image gave the emotion substance and validity, and Tara learned to respect the reality of it and stop trying to dismiss her anxiety as weakness or stupidity on her part.

As her understanding of herself deepened, the web softened, the color changed to match the shade of her skin. It gave us a vision we could share and a way for her to monitor her inner experience outside of our sessions. She began to take better care of herself and extended her circle of friends. She paid closer attention to her feelings and didn't get lost in thoughts about those feelings. She wore the threads of the original web as a cloak that brought her comfort when anxiety threatened.

Our work on Tara's anxiety borrowed language and technique from the imaginal world. In sorting out the issue, we exchanged an outmoded daydream—rational thought conquers all—for a new one—feelings are powerful allies. Our work reminded me of the way problems are solved in fairy tales where worldly and powerful figures find themselves and the kingdom in a crisis and can be saved only by an individual who had been previously overlooked, shunned or considered too simple to merit respect.

Daydreams create change. By using images, they introduce a new reality to the chemical and emotional processes of the mind-body and lead the way to the material manifestations of our hopes and wishes.

Returning

"Once upon a time, I, Chuang-tzu, dreamt I was a butterfly, flittering hither and thither, to all intents and purposes a butterfly . . . suddenly I awoke . . . Now I do not know whether I was then a man dreaming I was a butterfly, or whether I am now a butterfly dreaming I am a man."

—Chuang-tzu, Chinese philosopher

Integrating Dream Images

Every morning we return from the underworld of dreams and sleep. Brain waves shift. The busyness of the day reaches out to take possession of us. Don't just submit to the schedule's tyranny and impersonality. Bring the night's happenings with you.

We need not return empty-handed from our dreams. Often in the course of working on dreams, some aspect emerges as most salient. We can bring that image into waking life and integrate it into the concrete world.

Jane was a ballerina, a gentle, hardworking member of a professional company. She'd had several dreams involving guns: the buying and polishing of guns, being shot at, aiming a gun at someone else, a duel involving guns, and early morning violence. I suggested she find a firing range where she could explore guns in a safe setting. In her waking life, she'd never even been in the presence of a real gun, so with some trepidation, she drove to a large Quonset hut kind of building in the nearby suburbs. It was a Saturday morning, and she was the only woman on the scene.

Here's what happened.

Action in the light of a dream is a psychological obligation one owes to the Self. It may be done either practically or in the form of a ritual, itself a symbolic act.

     Anthony Stevens

"I looked at the models of guns shining in the glass case and asked the man about a pretty little .22. He explained that I'd need something more substantial out on the firing range and suggested a sturdy 96G, .40 caliber Beretta. All the while I could hear explosive hammerings of gunshot out in the range. I chose a paper target, handed over my driver's license in exchange for a gun and ammunition and earplugs. Trying to look like I knew what I was doing, I stepped into the half of the building that was the firing range. In the dim light, noise roared and rumbled. I went to an empty lane, hung my target, loaded my gun and began shooting.

"I was surprised to find that firing the gun felt good. It gave an outlet to an impulse I could just barely feel in myself: an aggression, an assertiveness. A concrete, focused urge to act. It was actually similar to the feeling I get before a performance. I pulled the trigger and added my sound to the crowded air. It was a voyage into my opposite, a stance I actually admire and, in a way, envy. Noise, fire, result. Cause and effect, aim and shoot. Just do it. In the dim light of the shooting range, I'd visited my own shadow, exercised it and experienced its power, beauty and lethalness."

Jane had ideas about society's relationship with firearms, but those ideas lived on a political, perhaps moral, level in her. The dreamworld, the unconscious, is several floors below those beliefs. It's important not to confuse the two. Dreams expand consciousness, and a consciously lived life will choose its own political positions.

In this set of dreams, the guns were equally symbols of aggression and symbols of efficacy. The dream and the dream work expanded her range of experience, gave her insight into the meanings firearms hold for people, and acquainted her with the pleasure, satisfaction and danger of holding a weapon in her hand. As a result, the world of firearms seems less alien to her. Increased consciousness always makes for connection, not division.

The symbolic acts that result from dream work are like rites and ceremonies. They are religious experiences of the most organic kind and can continue the changes initiated by the dreams. Images brought forward from dreams are powerful. One client incorporated images from dreams in a needlepoint sampler that told the story of a turbulent period in her life. Another, troubled by recurrent dreams of a long-dead, harsh grandmother, gave closure to the relationship by burying a toy figure in a corner of her backyard and planting daffodil bulbs over the site.

Another client used dream work to prepare for his retirement. At our first session, he reported this dream:

I had finished an important meeting and had my assistant call for the car. I took the elevator to the garage, but there was no sign of my driver. I tried my cell phone, but it wouldn't work. As I stood there waiting and getting really annoyed, I noticed a sleek black 1980 Z parked by the elevator. My roommate in college had had a Z, so I recognized it right away. I even walked over to it and ran my hand along the shiny, sloped roof. I couldn't take my eyes off it. I noticed it was unlocked. Then I awoke.

What is really important is the relationship of the dreamer to the dream, and that this relation should be kept alive as long as possible. . . .

━ ━ Dr. Sonya Marjasch

We worked on the dream together. I invited Thad to step back into the dream. Doing so, he noticed that the Z was the only car in the garage and that the place actually looked more like a showroom with low-focused lighting. The car door was indeed unlocked. He opened it, slid behind the wheel and relaxed into the soft black leather seat. It wasn't a new car. It had that broken-in, comfortable feeling. He felt very at-home there as if this had been his car for years.

Thad had enjoyed a very successful career in business. He came into therapy as he was beginning to consider retirement. The work just was no longer as fulfilling as it had been. He felt restless and a little frightened that the best years of his life were over. Because of his high position in his company, he had led a highly managed life. A driver appeared at his door in the morning and took him wherever he needed to go that day. Travel reservations were made for him. His wife shopped for his clothes and ran the house. Social events and golf games grew out of work connections. His well-ordered life sailed along, and he rarely had to interact with the guts of the machine, as it were. As retirement loomed, life as he knew it was about to change.

Much of Thad's success had come about in reaction to the awkwardness he'd felt as a kid. He wasn't good at sports, he had trouble staying on top of his studies, clubs and activities didn't appeal to him. When his friends nominated him for class president, he went along with the joke. To his surprise, he won the election and began a lifetime of "being good with people."

I suggested Thad spend some waking time with Zs before our next session. I recommended he look up articles about the car, visit a showroom—anything that would involve him with the image from the dream. That suggestion was all he needed. He dived into the project, test-drove a new model and found a mechanic who specialized in Zs. He talked about the experience.

"It was remarkable. You know, I know next to nothing about automobiles. That's not something I'm proud of. I just never could get interested, and I decided to make sure I earned enough money so that I could hire someone to do that for me. After my dream, I found a mechanic who specializes in Zs and spent a few hours on Saturday morning looking over his shoulder. I think I'm ready to get my hands dirty. It feels great."

Thad had returned from his dream with a perfect symbol for himself at this time of his life: highly valued, timeless, parked in a waiting area with the potential to go far, a perfect combination of pristine elegance and a greasy, dark, mysterious core. By spending time with the image in concrete reality, he was pursuing his own transformation. The more introverted, earthy and imaginative side of him began to stir again, this time supported by his maturity and experience.

In returning with enticing images, the dreamer populates his waking life with realities from his deepest core. By interacting with them,

It is very often the case that the dream suggests in images what the conscious life lacks or needs as a way of getting back into balance.

＾ℯ ＾ℯ Berger & Segaller

in Thad's case getting his hands dirty, he expands his identity and nourishes neglected hungers in himself. Our dreams remind us we are not only who we think we are or who we have been today and yesterday, but also that more self-development is always possible. This ongoing development introduces the infinite into our bounded lives.

For another client, the dream object was a copper au gratin pan. This was her dream.

I have returned to the house where I grew up. I walk through the kitchen doorway and find my mother standing at the stove stirring a pot. Next to it is an au gratin pan waiting to be filled and set in the oven. My mother looks very different—she is rounder and more contented than I remember her to be. She's dressed in a peasant skirt that reaches to the ground. And the stove isn't our old stove. It's a heavy black iron stove that connects right into the chimney there in the kitchen. My mother says to me, "Everything is different now."

Mary's mother had been dead for ten years, and Mary had come to understand their relationship with its strengths and weaknesses. Now in her 30s, she had accepted that her mother's sadness, anxiety and aloofness had nothing to do with her. So it was a great gift to encounter her mother transformed, peaceful and able to create warmth. Mary was particularly struck by the copper pan. Her mother would have never indulged herself with such a beautiful object. But as the dream-mother says, "Everything is different now."

So Mary went in search of a copper au gratin pan. She scanned catalogs and visited kitchen stores. It took some doing, but finally she found one at a garage sale that was oval shaped and the right size. She cooked herself nourishing meals in the pan and kept it on the stove to remind her that "everything is different now."

It interested her that the pan was made of copper. Any number of substances could have been sitting on that dream stove. Iron, aluminum, silver, pewter—all are used in cooking and serving food. Mary went off and read about copper, not in a dream dictionary but in an English dictionary and in a basic book on the elements. Those sources gave her facts that she could bring to her imaginal relationship with the au gratin pan. She learned that copper is known for its ability to conduct heat, for its malleability. It can move through a range of colors from a rosy-golden shade to a drab-green matte finish. It wears its constant interaction with human touch and the environment. The dream, the pan, the new aspects of her relationship with her mother: All acted as conduits of warmth and life to her. Seeing that stirred feelings of contentment and gratitude in her. Mary realized she herself was part copper: ever flexible, durable, changing and full of possibility.

The copper pan symbolized Mary's developing relationship with her mother and with her own feminine self. She was touched to feel her mother's new warmth at the same time that her own warmth was quickened by the encounter. Seeing the pot on her own stove reminded her of nourishing and being nourished. The beauty and sturdiness of the burnished copper enhanced Mary's grasp of her own beauty.

Don't be satisfied with stories,
how things have gone with
others. Unfold your own myth.

Rumi

The dream world is a timeless realm that exists in us even as we live with one eye on the clock. There, Mary's mother is not altered by death, but she does continue to develop, just as the relationship between Mary and her mother, and the relationship between Mary and the archetypal impulse of motherhood, goes on unfolding. In a psychological sense, it does not matter that Mary's mother is dead. Death is a matter of the rational, concrete world, but their essential relationship is timeless. This is not to say that death is easy for us who live to grieve our loved ones. As long as we populate the world of matter, death will insult and threaten and disrupt our lives.

But dreams like this one illustrate what Marie-Louise von Franz talks about in *On Dreams and Death:* "It is true . . . that the unconscious psyche pays very little attention to the abrupt end of bodily life and behaves as if the psychic life of the individual . . . will simply continue. . . . The unconscious 'believes' quite obviously in a life after death." This belief appears in dreams reported by the dying in which some sort of continuation is imaged along with, and beyond, the death of the body. I believe our dreams of the deceased also tap into that continuity.

Cultivating the Imaginal Mind

Dreams and dream work give us practice in the art of seeing more deeply and fully. They develop in us the imaginal mind that sees beyond literal reality into the living heart of everyday experience. A tree is a tree, and it can also be a home or a protector or a wise old soul. An auto is a method of conveyance. But it is also a chariot, an alter ego or an albatross. We are meaning-making creatures, and we naturally weave the internal and external to create the psychological world we live in.

For instance, think of a place you love. First, recall it with your senses. Imagine all those details that make it important to you: sights, sounds, textures, scents and maybe even tastes. Now, go a step further and identify the meaning this place has for you, the insubstantial but essential nature of it. What does it say to your soul? What part of your soul do you discover when you consider the place?

Our ability to see more deeply into things is like a sixth sense that rounds out our connection with the world and binds us to it more profoundly.

A young woman named Allie returned from a visit to California, deeply touched by a place across the Bay from San Francisco. She had hiked there and talked about the experience. I asked her to go deeper into that memory and see what meanings the place held for her. She thought for a minute, then said, "Well, when I think of Mt. Tamalpais, I feel held, nourished, as if a part of me that is hungry is being fed. Mt. Tamalpais means home, safety. In fact, the place is sort of like a mother to me. Does that sound too extreme? That's how it is. It's a place I can depend on for refuge and refreshment. I can be a carefree, well-looked-after kid when I'm there. Yes, that's how it is."

> *The dream's here still: even when*
> *I wake, it is*
> *Without me, as within me;*
> *not imagined, felt.*
>
> ∼ ∼ William Shakespeare

Allie is describing the meaning that animates this beautiful place for her. She is seeing deeper, past the material beauty of the place, into her unique relationship with it. The soul of the place speaks to her own soul, and it's her imaginal sense that enables her to experience it.

All our experiences carry that meaning load, although we are usually moving so quickly through our days that we don't have a chance to appreciate that. Let's say a family adopts a ginger-colored, long-haired kitten. Looking beyond the concrete facts of this kitten, which is named Starr, we would see a myriad of associations and meanings held by family members. To Mom, Starr is a sweet tie to her first pet, now long gone. To Dad, the feline threatens the order of the house and activates memories of a rambunctious classmate he disliked in high school. To the six-year-old son, Starr is pal and sibling and brings new possibilities to each morning's awakening. Starr is most certainly a mischievous ball of red fur, but she is also a deeper experience for each person in the house. And out of those deeper experiences, each individual's relationship with Starr takes on its own particular tone and hue, and each finds pleasure or discomfort in her presence.

> *Symbolic language is language in which the world outside is an image of the world inside, a symbol for our souls and our minds.*
>
> ～୧ ～୧ Erich Fromm

Our imaginal sensibility cues us to the currents of meaning always flowing through our material world. Because of it, life is animated and reanimated beyond its concrete dimensions. We are still dreamers in our waking hours, and the richest days weave together the worlds: earth and underworld, Kansas and Oz, the rational and the imaginal.

Back from the Beach

Earlier, I talked about my dream of the Neanderthal man. That dream, "A Day at the Beach," has accompanied me through the writing of this book. In my imagination, I visit the scene regularly, and it has become a place I go to rest, to stop thinking, to drop out of all kinds of "trying to." I sit in the sand, consider those long, straight lines, and still myself.

As a way of integrating the dream into my waking life, I bought sand and ball bearings and reproduced a small beach scene. I raked lines and scattered the balls among them. As I sit by the scene, I don't have blinding insights but I have had experience. I am calmed, quieted, even comfortable in its presence. The simplicity of shape and substance has settled into me, and I find myself believing more clearly in the value of the simple and straightforward. Creating that imaginal scene in my waking life has brought joy and a reminder that, yes, I'm not just writing a book about dreams, I am a dreamer. And like every other dreamer, I live in several consciousnesses.

Bringing the scene into my daytime world has challenged me to walk the walk, to act more consistently as though the imaginal world is real, and to allow its depth into my ordinary and practical living. When I sit at my desk, looking into the woods, I see not just the woods but a presence, other life, other processes—some like mine and some very different. I am learning about myself by really seeing into the place I have chosen for myself. Life is richer; more is possible.

The beach scene I've built is like a totem, a charm brought back from another country. When I look at it, I'm reminded that something beyond my waking consciousness created this scene. And I'm also reminded of James Hillman's words, "Our images are our keepers, as we are theirs." It is as though the beach image dreamed me into creating it in the day world.

Our dreams are practice runs at transformation, small imaginal growth spurts that infuse the material us with new life

The idea is to see every fragment of life and every dream as myth. . . . The images in events . . . give rise to meaningfulness, value, and the full range of experience.

       Thomas Moore

and direction. They, even more than the concrete world, are the home from which we emerge and to which we return in an endless cycle of being.

Appendix: Doing Dream Work

Here is a summary of the dream work tools I've discussed. Try various approaches to find what works most comfortably for you. The meaning comes last. It grows out of the experience of the dream and the time you spend with it. Meaning can come as a thought or an emotion. The key is to live with the dream and let it shape you.

Remember that as you focus on your dreams, you are tapping into the unknowns of the unconscious state. If you have concerns about doing so safely, check with a psychologist or social worker or counselor.

A Dream Work Guide

- Check for dreams on awakening. Recall and write or dictate the dream in as much detail as possible.
- Don't ask what the dream means. That comes later.
- Arrange to spend some uninterrupted time working with your dream. Establishing a routine time and place helps move you into the imaginal mind more easily.

- Admit you don't know what this dream means. If you think you do know, look again.
- Step back into the dream. Walk around. Observe the who, what, where, when and how that you find there. Note the emotions, the actions, and the body language. Notice what most draws you. If anything is distressing, take care to protect yourself so that you are free to safely observe what upsets you. Make notes.
- Notice what your dream self is doing and feeling. What part of yourself is the dream self showing you? How do you react to that?
- Does a title suggest itself? If this were a movie or a cartoon or a photo, what would you call it?
- What aspects of the dream particularly draw you? What's the felt sense you experience?
- Let your mind follow its associations. A person or object may remind you of another person or thing, another time or an emotion. Let those associations be part of the dream's story.
- Consider each element of the dream as an aspect of yourself. What are the various elements showing you? How does that feel? How does it sit with you? Notice if there is information you are resisting, and try to let it in.
- Take time to deepen your relaxation and initiate a conversation with an image from the dream. You can do this in your mind, in writing or by speaking the conversation into a tape recorder. What does the image have to say? What do you need to learn from it? What would you like to ask?
- Consult an English dictionary and other sources of fact—not interpretation—to learn more about the images in your dream.
- Talk with a friend about your dream. Speaking it aloud brings

insight and continues the experience.

- Consider all that the dream has brought to the fore for you. Perceive not just with your mind, but also with your heart, intuition and imagination. What is the new information the dream has stirred in you? It may dazzle or it may feel small and quiet. Allow it to seep in. Live with it, try it out in the daytime world. Revisit the dream at another time and notice what you see once it has been leavened by waking experiences.

- Watch for opportunities to integrate images from the dream into daily life.

The dream is the small hidden door in the deepest and most intimate sanctum of the soul, which opens into that primeval cosmic night that was soul long before there was a conscious ego and will be soul far beyond what a conscious ego could ever reach.

— C. G. Jung

Reference Reading

The Alphabet Versus the Goddess, Leonard Shlain

Animal Life in Nature, Myth and Dreams, Elizabeth Caspari

Archetypal Dimensions of the Psyche, Marie-Louise von Franz

Awakening Intuition, Frances E. Vaughan

Awakening the Heart, John Welwood

A Blue Fire, edited by Thomas Moore

The Committee of Sleep, Deidre Barret, PhD

The Cry for Myth, Rollo May

Daydreaming, Jerome L. Singer

Dreaming, edited by Barbara Tedlock

Dreams Are Wiser than Men, edited by Richard Russo

Dreamscaping, edited by Stanley Krippner, PhD, and Mark Robert Waldman

The Dynamics of Symbols, Verena Kast

The Forgotten Language, Erich Fromm

Getting a Grip on Dreams, Maeve Ennis and Jennifer Parker

In the House of Night, edited by Christopher Navrati

Jung and the Alchemical Imagination, Jeffrey Raff

Jung and Tarot, Sallie Nichols

Jung and the Post-Jungians, Andrew Samuels

Jungian Dream Interpretation, James A. Hall, MD

Jungian Psychology Unplugged, Daryl Sharp

A Life of Jung, Ronald Hayman

Living Myth, D. Stephenson Bond

Memories, Dreams, Reflections, C. G.Jung

Night: Night Life, Night Language, Sleep and Dreams, A. Alvarez

On Dreams and Death, Marie-Louise von Franz

Our Dreaming Mind, Robert L. Van de Castle, PhD

The Poetics of Space, Gaston Bachelard

The Portable Jung, Carl G. Jung; edited by Joseph Campbell

Private Myths: Dreams and Dreaming, Anthony Stevens

Psyche and Matter, Marie-Louise von Franz

Revisioning Psychology, James Hillman

"Smaller than Small, Bigger than Big: The Little Dream's Role in Inner Growth" from *Dreams, Dreamers and Dreaming*, Stephen Martin, PsyD

The Symbolic Quest, Edward C. Whitmont

The Two Million-Year-Old Self, Anthony Stevens

The Wisdom of the Dream, Merrill Berger and Stephen Segaller

Where People Fly and Water Runs Uphill, Jeremy Taylor

Writers Dreaming, Naomi Epel

Your Mythic Journey, Sam Keen and Anne Valley-Fox

Acknowledgments

No one writes a book alone.

My thanks begin with appreciation to Elisabeth Rinaldi, whose dream "Alligators Under the Bed" inspired this project. Thanks to Elisabeth, Michele Matrisciani, and Andrea Gold, my editors, who offered insightful editing and welcome encouragement.

My colleagues of 30 South Writers, Barbara Crawford and Steve Oskie, have shared their own creative talents in our discussions about the book in its several revisions. My thanks to them for their love of words and ideas and their absolutely dependable, generous support.

My readers very kindly gave time and energy to read and reflect on the first draft and served as audience and cheering section as I wrote. Thank you all: Celeste Aliberti, LCSW; Tina Bela Limer; Dorothy Burton, MS; Dr. Karen Clark-Schock; Barbara Crawford; Tina Devine; Elinor Donohue; Joanne Mazzeo; Liz Mohamed; Katherine Mooney; Steve Oskie; Dr. Steve Martin; and Mary Shields.

I am grateful, too, to Sandy Yunkin for her smart and efficient work in doing research and in managing the clerical aspects of the project.

And special thanks to all the dreamers who have shared the images and stories of their nights.

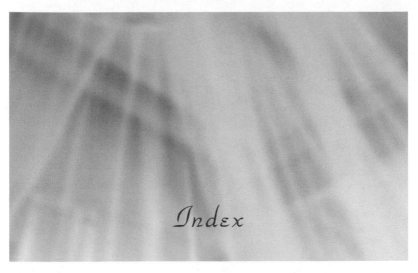

Index

A
active imagination, 63–67
amygdaloid complex, 70
archetypes, 40–41, 79
Artemedorus, 7
arts, numinosity of, 35
Aserinsky, Eugene, 21

B
Baraka, 56–57
benzene molecule, structure of, 10
Berger, Merrill, 83–84
Bergman, Ingmar, 10
Bible
    New Testament, 9
    Old Testament, 8–9, 32
biofeedback, 97–98
body, soul and, 26
Bosnak, Robert, 63
brain
    emotional center of, 70
    image as storage mechanism in, 34
    left and right, 28–29
    operation of during sleep, 21–22
Buddha, 11
Buddhism, 8

C
Cartwright, Rosalind, 79
childhood, imagination in, 29–30
Children Dreaming (Mallon), 20

Christianity, view of dreams, 8–9
Church of Jesus Christ of Latter Day
    Saints, 11
collective unconscious, 19
communication, with images, 33–34
consciousness, 50
court jester, as archetype, 14–15,
    41–43
creativity, dreams and, 9–10
cultural daydreams, 94
cultural mythology, 35–38
cultural resistance, 13–14

D
Daydreaming (Singer), 89
daydreams, 88–90, 91–93
    cultural or shared, 94
    healing with, 95–97
    pain management and, 97–98
    See also dreams
Demeter, 35–37
dream interpretation, history of, 7–12
dream work
    dialogues in, 63
    entering the dream, 57–63
    establishing, 55–56
    guide to, 115–117
    practicing, 15–16, 44–48
dreams
    ambivalence about, 13
    archetypal, 40–41

context of, 23–24
creativity and, 9–10
cultural resistance to, 13–14
emotion expressed in, 70–78
as form of communication
    between psyche and ego, 24–25
integration of into everyday life,
    104–110
as metaphors, 60
origins of, 18–20
precognitive, 11
public, 38
as reality check, 14–15
recollection of, 55–56
recurrent, 78–84
as revelations of hidden traits and
    feelings, 51–54
scientific exploration of, 21–23
scientific thought and, 10
spirituality and, 7–8
synchronicity and, 84–86
use of imaginal to personify reality
    in, 39–44
witchcraft and, 9
See also daydreams; fantasies;
    nightmares
Dreams (Kurosawa), 34–35

E
ego, 24–25, 26
emotions, expression of in dreams,
    70–78
Ennis, Maeve, 72
ethical behavior, 53
Euridyce, 50
"Exploring Our Fears of the
    Paranormal" (Tart), 13

F
fantasies, 93–94
    See also daydreams; dreams
felt sense, 77–78
Ferdinand, Archduke, 11
Frankenstein (Shelley), 10
Franz, Marie-Louise von, 110
Freud, Sigmund, 7, 19
"Future of Energetic Healing, The"
    (Tart), 13

G
Gandhi, 10
Gendlin, Eugene, 77
Getting a Grip on Dreams (Ennis &
    Parker), 72
God
    collective unconscious as, 19
    as higher power, 26
    as originator of dreams., 32
    spiritual mythology and, 38
    guided imagery, 95–96

H
healing nightmares, 84
hearts, symbolism of, 31–32
Herod, 9
higher power, God as, 26
Hillman, James, 113
Howdy Doody, 22–23
Howe, Elias, 10
humanity, defining, 25

I
images, communication by, 33–34
imaginal world
    cultivation of, 110–112
    during sleep, 38–44
    language in, 34, 39
    waking hours, 31–38
imagination
    active, 63–67
    in childhood, 29–30
incubus, 9
Interpretation of Dreams, The
    (Artemedorus), 7
Interpretation of Dreams, The (Freud), 7
International Association for the
    Study of Dreams, 20
International Remote Viewing
    Association, 12

J
Jerome, 9
Jesus, 9
Johns, Jasper, 10
Johnson, Lyndon, 11
Jonah (Old Testament), 32
Joseph (New Testament), 9

Joseph (Old Testament), 8–9
Jung and Tarot: An Archetypal Journey (Nichols), 43
Jung, C. G., 7, 14, 19, 24, 39, 40

K
Kafka, Franz, 10
Kekule, Friedrich A. von, 10
Kerouac, Jack, 10
King Lear (Shakespeare), 15
Kleitman, Nathaniel, 21
Kurosawa, Akira, 34–35

L
ladder, as metaphor for dream connections, 8–9
language, imaginal, 34, 39
Lanyi, Joseph, 11
Lincoln, Abraham, 11
logic, 28

M
Mallon, Brenda, 20
Mansfield, Kathryn, 10
Mendeleyev, Dmitri, 10
metaphors, 29
Midsummer Night's Dream, A (Shakespeare), 43
mythology. See cultural mythology; personal myths

N
Nichols, Sallie, 43
nightmares, 72, 74–77
    healing, 84
NREM sleep, 21
numinosity, 31, 35

O
On Dreams and Death (von Franz), 110
Orpheus, 50
Our Dreaming Mind (Van de Castle), 7, 78

P
pain, management of with conscious daydreams, 97–98
paranormal modes of perception, 12
paranormal research, 13
parapsychological activity. See psi activity
Parker, Jennifer, 72
Patton, Gen. George, 11
Paul, Saint, 9
perception, paranormal modes of, 12
period table of elements, 10
Persephone, 36–37
personal myths, 79
Peter Pan Syndrome, 36
Peter, Saint, 9
Post-Traumatic Stress Disorder, 83–84
precognition, 11–12
precognitive dreams, 11
Private Myths: Dreams and Dreaming (Stevens), 14, 21
psi activity, 11–12, 13
psyche, 24, 60
psychology, transpersonal, 26
public dreams, 38
Puck, 43
Puthoff, Hal, 12

Q
quantum science, 53

R
rationality, 28, 53–54
reality, personification of, 39–44
recurrent dreams, 78–84
religion. See spirituality
REM sleep, 21–22
Remote Viewing, 12

S
Sawdust and Tinsel (Bergman), 10
science, dreams and, 10
Segaller, Stephen, 83–84
Shakespeare, William, 15, 43
shared daydreams, 94
Shelley, Mary, 10
Singer, Jerome, 89

sleep
   Non-Rapid Eye Movement
      (NREM), 21
   operation of brain during, 21–22
   Rapid Eye Movement (REM),
      21–22
Smith, Buffalo Bob, 23
Smith, Joseph, 11
social mythology, 38
soul, body and, 26
spiritual mythology, 38
spirituality, 26
   dreams and, 7–8
   numinosity in, 35
Stevens, Anthony, 14, 21, 74–75
Stevenson, Robert Louis, 10
Strange Case of Dr. Jekyll and Mr. Hyde,
   The (Stevenson), 10
stream of consciousness, 90–91
succubus, 9
Sufis, 8
Summa Theologica (Thomas Aquinas),
   9
synchronicity, 84–86

T
Tart, Charles T., 13
Taylor, Jeremy, 79
Thomas Aquinas, 9
transcendence, 12–13
transpersonal psychology, 26
truth, revealed in dreams, 14–15
Tubman, Harriet, 10

U
unconscious, 19, 50, 54, 84–85
Underground Railroad, 10
Upanishads, 8

V
Van de Castle, Robert L., 7, 78
Vedas, 8
Vietnam War, 11
visualization, 99–101

W
Warren, Robert Penn, 10
Wild Strawberries (Bergman), 10
Wilmer, Dr. Harry, 84
Wisdom of the Dream, The (Berger
    & Segaller), 83–84
witchcraft, dreams and, 9
World War I, 11

About the Author

Emma Mellon, PhD, is a licensed psychologist in private practice in Berwyn, Pennsylvania. Dr. Mellon teaches and lectures on a variety of psychological issues. In addition to clinical work, she writes nonfiction and poetry. She is currently at work on a memoir about her years with her first dog, a retired greyhound. She dreams regularly.

You can visit her website at www.*emmamellonphd*.com.

The Velveteen Principles

A Guide to Becoming Real

Hidden Wisdom from a Children's Classic

Toni Raiten-D'Antonio

Code #2114 • hardcover • $14.95

Let the wisdom of a children's classic lead
you to a life of love, fulfillment and purpose.
